MODERN

Getting Ready for Preschool
GIANT BASIC SKILLS™
Workbook

D1474460

Modern Publishing
A Division of Unisystems, Inc.
New York, New York 10022
Series UPC: 49130

This book
belongs to:

....

Illustrated by Arthur Friedman
Educational Consultants: Shereen Gertel Rutman, M.S.
Mary Mclean Hely, M.A. in Education, Design and Evaluation of Educational Programs
Colorization and page design by Creative Quotient

To the Parents

Dear Parents,

As your child's first and most important teacher, you can encourage your child's love of learning by participating in educational activities at home. Working together on the activities in this workbook will help your child build confidence, learn to reason, and develop skills necessary for early childhood education.

The following are some suggestions to help make your time together enjoyable and rewarding.

▶ Choose a time when you and your child are relaxed.

▶ Provide a writing tool that your child is familiar with.

▶ Don't attempt to do too many pages at one time or expect that every page be completed. Move on if your child is frustrated or loses interest.

▶ Discuss each page. Help your child relate the concepts in this book to everyday experiences.

▶ Encourage your child to use the practice pages provided at the end of the LEARNING LETTERS, NUMBER CONCEPTS, and WORKING WITH NUMBERS sections to work independently and reinforce skills.

▶ Use the Achievement Checklist to keep track of the pages you need to revisit. When the "Mastered" column is full, your child has earned the diploma at the back of the book!

Happy Learning!

Essential Skills

The repetitive activities within each chapter have been designed to help children learn the organizational skills necessary for learning and thinking.

CHAPTER 1 BEGINNING WRITING SKILLS

Learning to control the small muscles of the hand **(fine motor skill development)** allows the child to make the precise movements necessary for forming letters, while activities such as **writing from left to right, tracing,** and **forming lines** help to refine eye-hand coordination.

CHAPTER 2 LEARNING LETTERS

Children practice **tracing and writing letters** and recognizing which **uppercase and lowercase letters** go together.

CHAPTER 3 READING READINESS

Before learning to read, children must be able to distinguish **same and different.** For example, children usually recognize the difference between a cow and a horse before they recognize different letters. The emphasis in this chapter is on various visual skills, including **noticing details, comparing, matching figures,** and **understanding directionality.**

FIRST WORD BOOK

This special section presents scenes familiar to young children, with word labels to help build **sight vocabulary.** After mastering the labeled words, children are invited to add their own words to each category.

CHAPTER 4 BEGINNING PHONICS

After practicing making **visual distinctions,** children can use visual and auditory discrimination to **recognize and reproduce initial and final consonant sounds.**

CHAPTER 5 WORDS THAT RHYME

Children identify picture words and determine which words rhyme. **Word families** serve as an example of **rhyming words** that are spelled in a similar way.

CHAPTER 6 COLORS AND SHAPES

Grouping things according to common attributes such as color, size, shape, etc. **(classification activities)** encourages development of a child's ability to reason and make **logical connections.**

CHAPTER 7 MATH READINESS SKILLS

By **observing, reproducing, and continuing patterns,** children develop **visual memory** skills, which prepare them for learning to recognize numbers. Various activities that focus on **making comparisons** also aid in the development of **number sense** and an understanding of **mathematical order.**

CHAPTER 8 NUMBER CONCEPTS

The emphasis in this chapter is on **identifying** and **creating sets of objects and their corresponding numerals,** and on **recognizing numerals and number words.** These activities prepare children for basic math.

CHAPTER 9 WORKING WITH NUMBERS

Becoming familiar with the **order of numbers from 1 to 10, learning to write numbers,** and **understanding the connection between a set of objects and its corresponding numeral** all prepare a child to understand the concepts of addition and subtraction.

Table of Contents

Beginning Writing Skills

Trace the broken lines. Color the pictures.

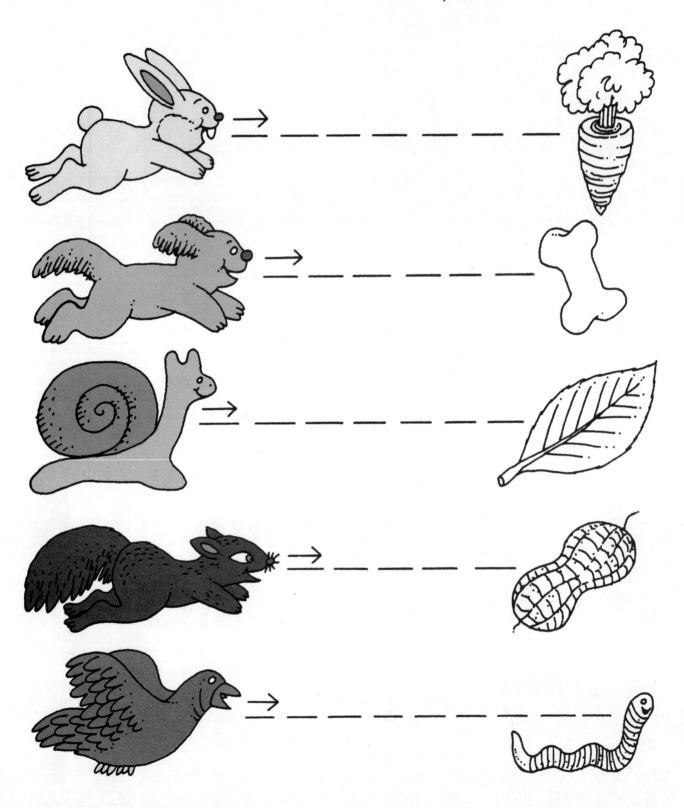

Skills: Writing from left to right; Association; Fine motor skill development

Beginning Writing Skills

Trace the broken lines. Color the pictures.

Skills: Fine motor skill development; Eye/hand coordination

9

Trace and color the picture.

Skills: Fine motor skill development; Eye/hand coordination

Beginning Writing Skills

Start at the dots. Trace the broken lines.

Skills: Fine motor skill development; Eye/hand coordination; Forming vertical lines

Start at the dots. Trace the broken lines.

Skills: Fine motor skill development; Eye/hand coordination; Forming diagonal lines

Start at the dots. Trace the broken lines.

Skills: Fine motor skill development; Eye/hand coordination; Forming diagonal lines

Beginning Writing Skills

Start at the dots. Trace the broken lines.

Skills: Fine motor skill development; Eye/hand coordination; Forming diagonal lines

Start at the dots. Trace the broken lines.

Skills: Fine motor skill development; Eye/hand coordination; Forming open curves

Start at the dots. Trace the broken lines.

Skills: Fine motor skill development; Eye/hand coordination; Forming open curves

Beginning Writing Skills

Trace the broken lines.

Skills: Fine motor skill development; Eye/hand coordination; Forming closed curves

Beginning Writing Skills

Start at the dots. Trace the broken lines.

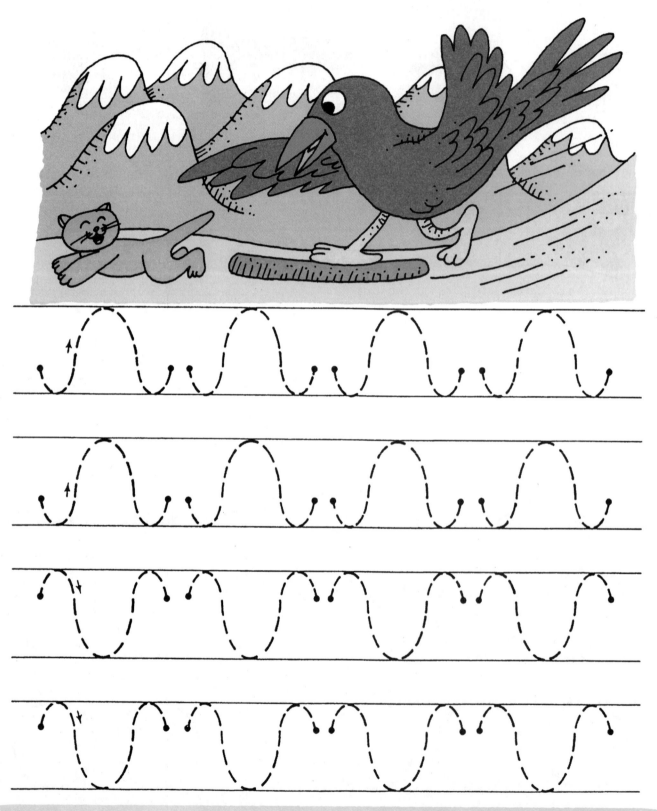

Skills: Fine motor skill development; Eye/hand coordination; Forming open curves

18

Beginning Writing Skills

Start at the dots. Trace the broken lines. Finish the page.

Beginning Writing Skills

Start at the dots. Trace the broken lines. Finish the page.

Skills: Fine motor skill development; Eye/hand coordination; Forming horizontal lines

Excellent!

Give yourself a star!

Learning
Letters

Aa

Follow the direction of each arrow. Then practice writing each letter.
Point to something in the picture that begins with A.

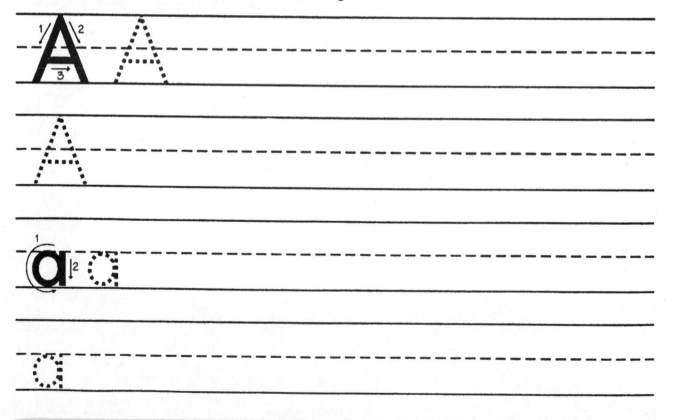

Skills: Forming upper/lowercase "a"; Writing left to right

Bb

Follow the direction of each arrow. Then practice writing each letter.
Point to something in the picture that begins with B.

Cc

Follow the direction of each arrow. Then practice writing each letter.
Point to something in the picture that begins with C.

Skills: Forming upper/lowercase "c"; Writing left to right

Learning Letters

Dd

Follow the direction of each arrow. Then practice writing each letter.
Point to something in the picture that begins with D.

Skills: Forming upper/lowercase "d"; Writing left to right

27

Ee

Follow the direction of each arrow. Then practice writing each letter.
Point to something in the picture that begins with E.

Skills: Forming upper/lowercase "e"; Writing left to right

Ff

Follow the direction of each arrow. Then practice writing each letter.
Point to something in the picture that begins with F.

Gg

Follow the direction of each arrow. Then practice writing each letter.
Point to something in the picture that begins with G.

Skills: Forming upper/lowercase "g"; Writing left to right

30

Hh

Follow the direction of each arrow. Then practice writing each letter.
Point to something in the picture that begins with H.

Skills: Forming upper/lowercase "h"; Writing left to right

I i

Follow the direction of each arrow. Then practice writing each letter.
Point to something in the picture that begins with I.

Jj

Follow the direction of each arrow. Then practice writing each letter. Point to something in the picture that begins with J.

Skills: Forming upper/lowercase "j"; Writing left to right

Follow the direction of each arrow. Then practice writing each letter.
Point to something in the picture that begins with K.

Skills: Forming upper/lowercase "k"; Writing left to right

L l

Follow the direction of each arrow. Then practice writing each letter.
Point to something in the picture that begins with L.

Mm

Follow the direction of each arrow. Then practice writing each letter.
Point to something in the picture that begins with M.

Skills: Forming upper/lowercase "m"; Writing left to right

Nn

Follow the direction of each arrow. Then practice writing each letter.
Point to something in the picture that begins with N.

Follow the direction of each arrow. Then practice writing each letter.
Point to something in the picture that begins with O.

Skills: Forming upper/lowercase "o"; Writing left to right

P p

Follow the direction of each arrow. Then practice writing each letter.
Point to something in the picture that begins with P.

Follow the direction of each arrow. Then practice writing each letter.
Point to something in the picture that begins with Q.

Skills: Forming upper/lowercase "q"; Writing left to right

R r

Follow the direction of each arrow. Then practice writing each letter.
Point to something in the picture that begins with R.

Skills: Forming upper/lowercase "r"; Writing left to right

Ss

Follow the direction of each arrow. Then practice writing each letter.
Point to something in the picture that begins with S.

S S

S

S S

S

Skills: Forming upper/lowercase "s"; Writing left to right

Learning Letters

T t

Follow the direction of each arrow. Then practice writing each letter.
Point to something in the picture that begins with T.

Skills: Forming upper/lowercase "t"; Writing left to right

43

Follow the direction of each arrow. Then practice writing each letter. Point to something in the picture that begins with U.

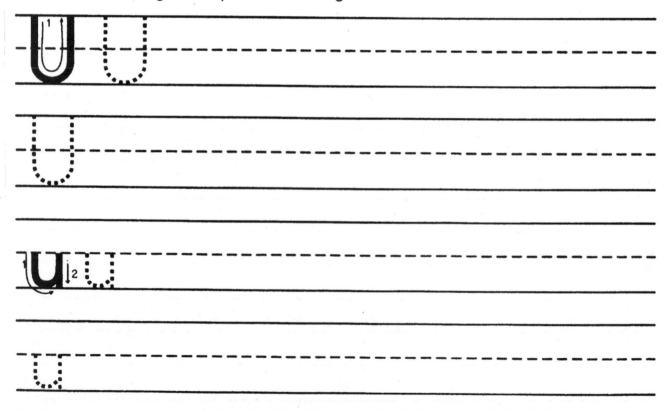

V v

Follow the direction of each arrow. Then practice writing each letter.
Point to something in the picture that begins with V.

W w

Follow the direction of each arrow. Then practice writing each letter. Point to something in the picture that begins with W.

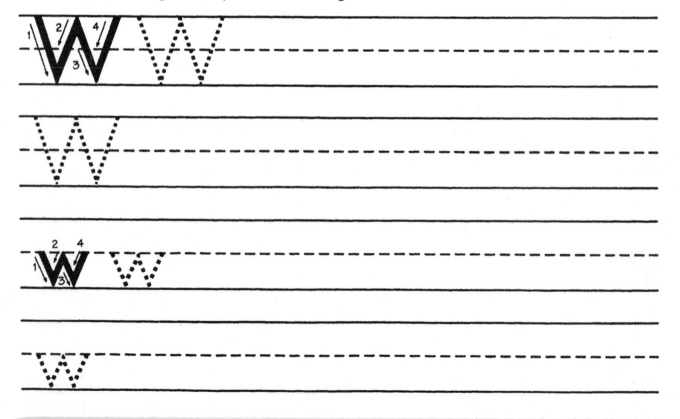

Skills: Forming upper/lowercase "w"; Writing left to right

X x

Follow the direction of each arrow. Then practice writing each letter.
Point to something in the picture that begins with X.

Skills: Forming upper/lowercase "x"; Writing left to right

Y y

Follow the direction of each arrow. Then practice writing each letter.
Point to something in the picture that begins with Y.

Skills: Forming upper/lowercase "y"; Writing left to right

Zz

Follow the direction of each arrow. Then practice writing each letter.
Point to something in the picture that begins with Z.

Skills: Forming upper/lowercase "z"; Writing left to right

Connect the dots from a to z to find out what is growing in the park.
Then color the picture.

Skills: Letter order; Recognition of lowercase letters

Practice Page

Use these pages to practice writing letters.

Practice Page

Well Done!

Give
yourself
a star!

Reading
Readiness

Reading Readiness

Look at each picture. Draw a line to match the pictures that look the same.

Skills: Visual discrimination; Matching like figures

Color the pictures in each row that are the same.

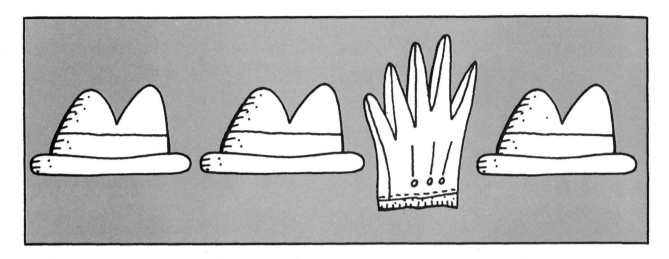

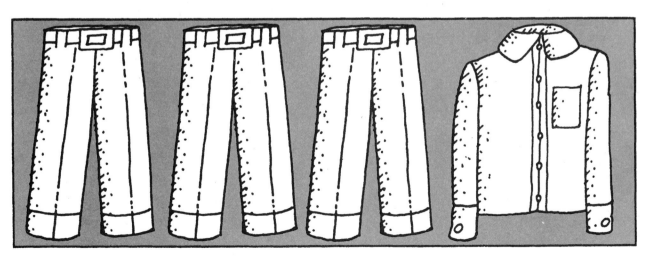

Skills: Visual discrimination; Matching like figures

Reading Readiness

Look at the pictures.
Draw a line from **each** animal to its home.

Skills: Association; Classification; Logical reasoning

Reading Readiness

Match the picture of each mother to her baby.

Reading Readiness

Color the three pictures in each box that go together.

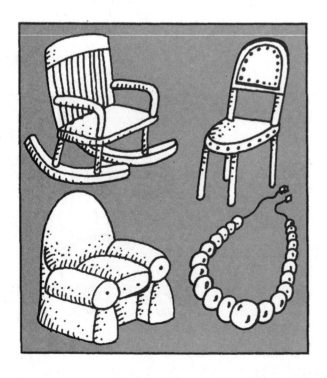

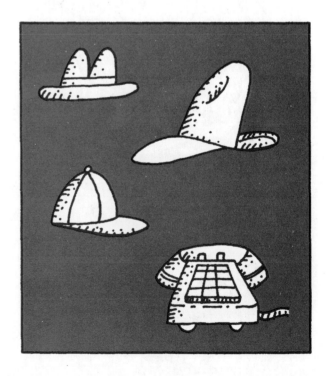

Skills: Association; Classification; Logical reasoning

Look at each picture. Something is missing.
Circle the picture that is different.

Skills: Visual discrimination; Noticing details; Following directions

Look at each picture. Which ones make music?
Color the pictures of musical instruments.

Skills: Association; Classification; Logical reasoning

Color the two pictures in **each** box that go together.

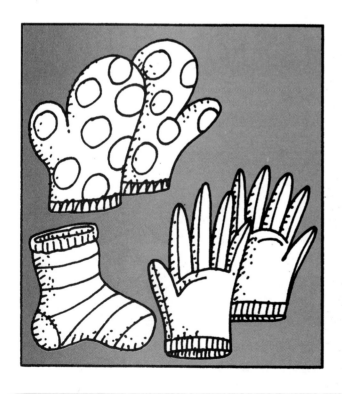

Skills: Association; Classification; Logical reasoning

Reading Readiness

Look at the pictures in each row.
Circle the picture that goes in a different direction from the others.
Then color the pictures.

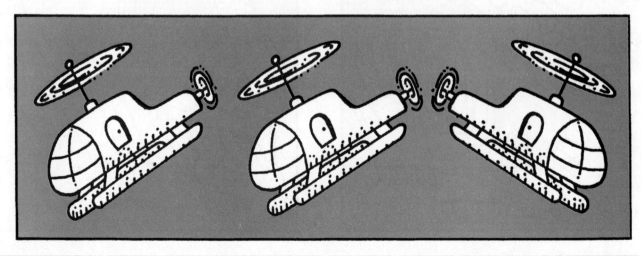

Skills: Visual discrimination; Understanding directionality; Following directions

Reading Readiness

Look at the pictures in each row.
Circle the picture that goes in a different direction from the others.
Then color the pictures.

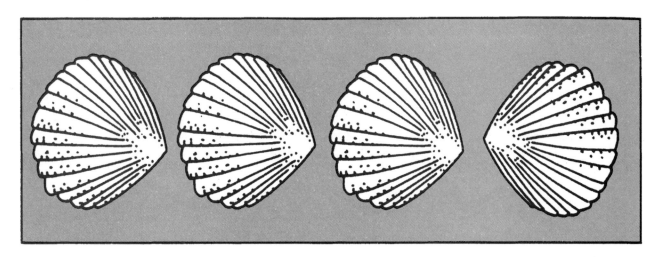

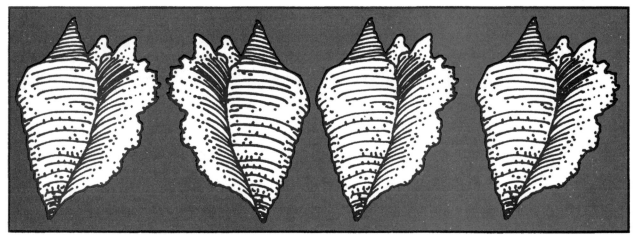

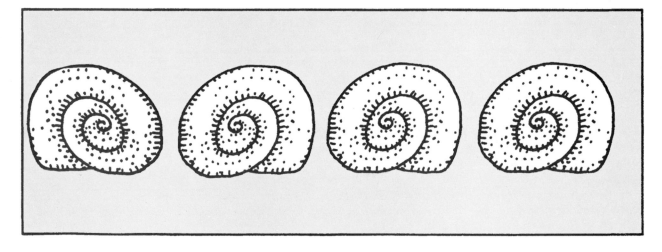

Skills: Visual discrimination; Understanding directionality; Following directions

Reading Readiness

Look at the pictures in each row.
Circle the picture that goes in a different direction from the others.
Then color the pictures.

Skills: Visual discrimination; Understanding directionality; Following directions

Reading Readiness

Look at the pictures in each row.
Circle the picture that goes in a different direction from the others.
Then color the pictures.

Skills: Visual discrimination; Understanding directionality; Following directions

Reading Readiness

The fish at the top of the page is facing right.
Look at the rest of the pictures.
Color the pictures that show fish facing right.

right

Skills: Visual discrimination; Understanding directionality; Following directions

The snail at the top of the page is facing left.
Look at the rest of the pictures.
Circle the pictures that show snails facing left.

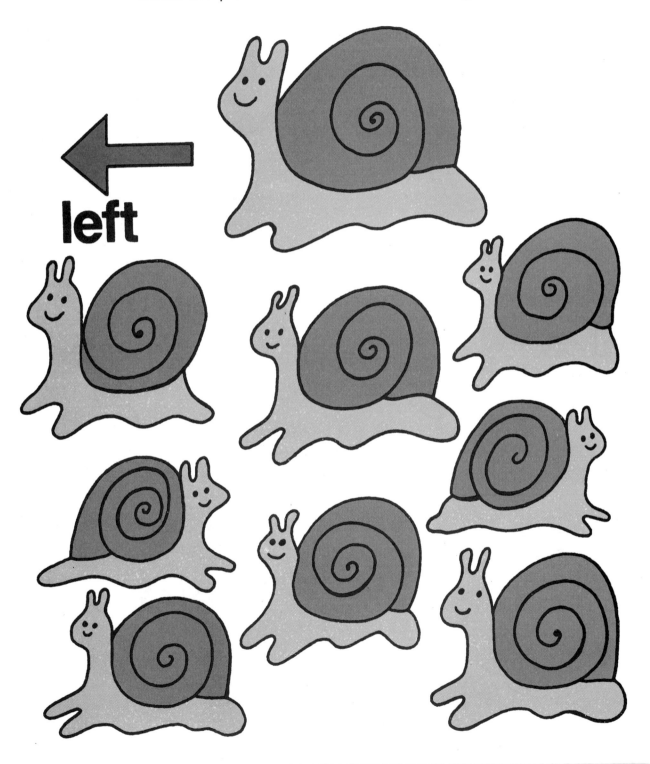

left

Skills: Recognizing directionality; Word recognition

Reading Readiness

Look at the pictures at the top of this page.
One bird is facing left. One bird is facing right.
Then look at the rest of the pictures.
Circle the pictures that show animals facing left.
Draw a line under the pictures that show animals facing right.

left

right

Look at the pictures.
Draw a line between the pictures that are opposites.

Skills: Vocabulary; Opposites

Reading Readiness

Look at the pictures.
Draw a line between the pictures that are opposites.

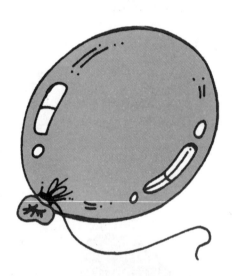

Reading Readiness

Look at the socks on the clotheslines.
Sort them into pairs by drawing a line between the matching socks.
Then color the page.

Skills: Understanding pairs; Visual matching

Reading Readiness

Look at the mittens on this page. Draw lines to match each pair.
Then color each pair a different color.

Reading Readiness

Look at the pattern in each row.
Circle a picture at the end of each row that continues the pattern.
Then color the pictures.

Skills: Observing and continuing patterns

Reading Readiness

Look at the pattern in each row.
Circle a picture at the end of each row that continues the pattern.
Then color the pictures.

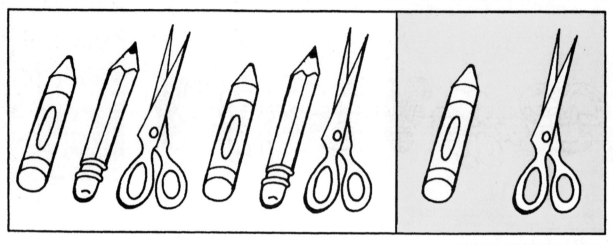

Skills: Observing and continuing patterns

Help the cat find her kittens.

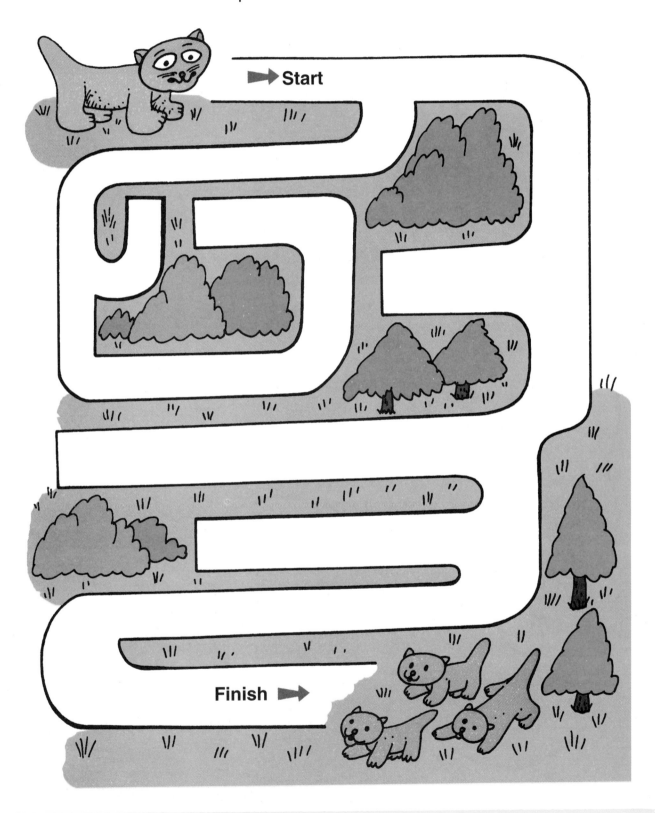

Start

Finish

Skills: Visual perception; Fine motor skill development

Reading Readiness

Help these children find their way to school.

Start

Finish

SCHOOL

Skills: Visual perception; Fine motor skill development

Here are some foods you might like to eat. Look carefully at each food.
When you are ready, turn the page to play a memory game.

Skills: Visual memory; Association; Following directions

Reading Readiness

Look at the pictures on this page.
Which ones do you remember from the last page?
Circle the ones you remember. Then color all of the pictures.

Skills: Visual memory; Association; Following directions

Good Job!

Give
yourself
a star!

First Word Book

First Word Book

Look at me!

Skills: Identifying objects; Building vocabulary

Can you name other parts of your body?

head

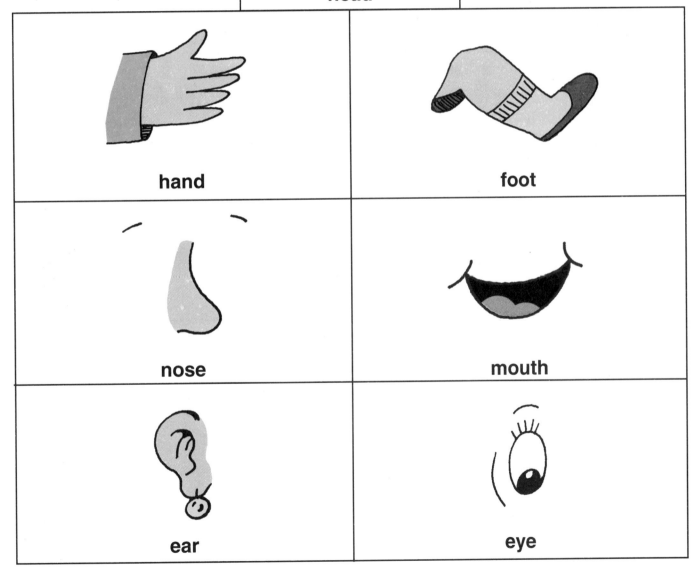

hand

foot

nose

mouth

ear

eye

Skills: Identifying objects; Building vocabulary

Our Family

mother

father

sister

brother

Skills: Identifying objects; Building vocabulary

Who is in your family?

grandmother

grandfather

baby

dog

Skills: Identifying objects; Building vocabulary

In My Room

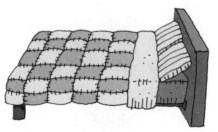

bed

dresser

chair

doll

Skills: Identifying objects; Building vocabulary

What else do you see in the picture?

books

desk

lamp

teddy bear

Skills: Identifying objects; Building vocabulary

Our Dinner Table

glass

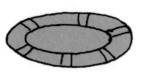

plate

fork

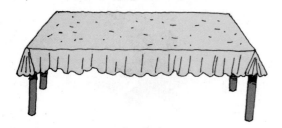

table

bowl

Skills: Identifying objects; Building vocabulary

First Word Book

Name some things you like to eat.

spoon

knife

napkin

chair

Skills: Identifying objects; Building vocabulary

At My School

chalkboard

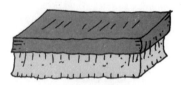

eraser

scissors

crayons

Skills: Identifying objects; Building vocabulary

First Word Book

What else do you see in the picture?

paper

pencil

teacher

paints

paste

In the Park

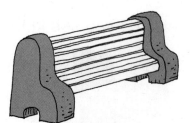

bench

see-saw

slide

water fountain

Skills: Identifying objects; Building vocabulary

swings

What else do you see in the picture?

sandbox

ball

bicycle

Skills: Identifying objects; Building vocabulary

At the Grocery Store

cart

can

apple

bread

basket

Skills: Identifying objects; Building vocabulary

What else do you see in the picture?

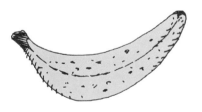

banana

cash register

milk

bag

eggs

Skills: Identifying objects; Building vocabulary

At the Mall

gloves

coat

pants

shirt

Skills: Identifying objects; Building vocabulary

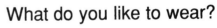

What do you like to wear?

sweater

shoes

dress

socks

Skills: Identifying objects; Building vocabulary

At the Doctor's Office

doctor

nurse

stethoscope

crutches

Skills: Identifying objects; Building vocabulary

First Word Book

patient

thermometer

What else do you see in the doctor's office?

bandage

scale

Skills: Identifying objects; Building vocabulary

In the City

building

traffic light

mailbox

garbage can

Skills: Identifying objects; Building vocabulary

First Word Book

What else do you see in the picture?

taxi

bus

stop sign

shopping bag

Skills: Identifying objects; Building vocabulary

On the Farm

barn

horse

corn

cow

pumpkins

Skills: Identifying objects; Building vocabulary

First Word Book

What else do you see in the picture?

pig

chicken

cat

hay

tractor

Skills: Identifying objects; Building vocabulary

At the Zoo

monkey

snake

seal

polar bear

giraffe

Skills: Identifying objects; Building vocabulary

First Word Book

Name some animals you have seen at the zoo.

zebra

elephant

penguin

lion

Skills: Identifying objects; Building vocabulary

In the Bathroom

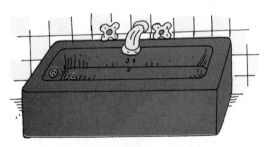

tub

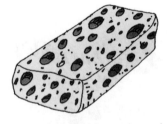

sponge

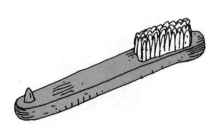

toothbrush

toothpaste

Skills: Identifying objects; Building vocabulary

What else do you see in the picture?

soap

sink

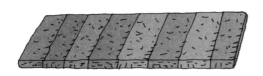

mat

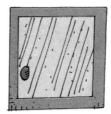

mirror

Skills: Identifying objects; Building vocabulary

At the Beach

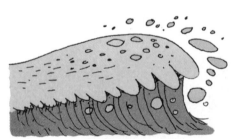

wave

sand castle

shell

umbrella

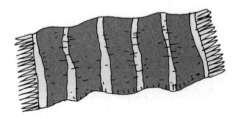

towel

Skills: Identifying objects; Building vocabulary

What else do you see in the **picture**?

pail

shovel

lifeguard

sun

Skills: Identifying objects; Building vocabulary

First Word Book

A Winter Wonderland

mittens

skates

boots

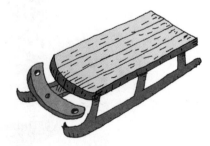

sled

skis

Skills: Identifying objects; Building vocabulary

What else do you see in the picture?

snowman

snowball

scarf

hat

Skills: Identifying objects; Building vocabulary

A Birthday Party

crown

balloons

party hat

presents

Skills: Identifying objects; Building vocabulary

What do you do on your birthday?

cake

friends

candles

game

candy

Skills: Identifying objects; Building vocabulary

Where do you like to go? Draw a picture of a place you like to be.

Then ask someone to help you write words to go with your picture.

Excellent!

Give
yourself
a star!

Beginning
Phonics

Beginning Phonics

The "b" sound

Bb

Which ones begin with b? Color them blue.

Skills: Recognition of the "b" sound; Sound/symbol association

The "d" sound

Dd

Which ones begin with d? Color them red.

Skills: Recognition of the "d" sound; Sound/symbol association

The "f" sound

Ff

Which ones begin with f? Color them red.

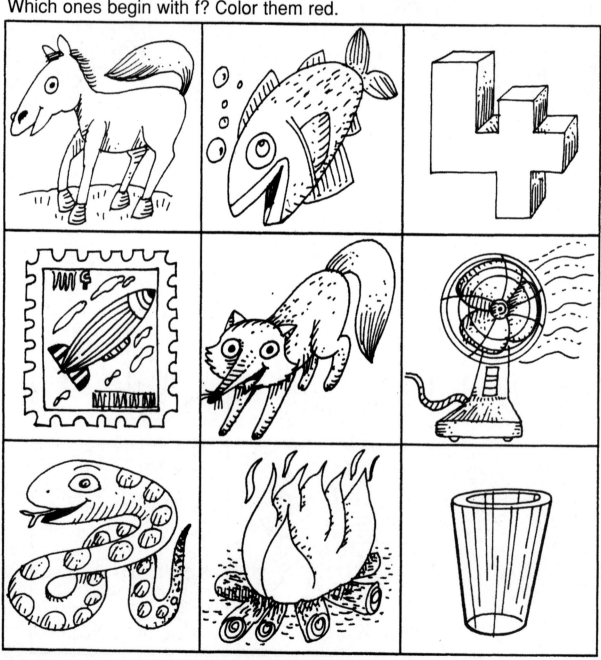

The "g" sound

Which ones begin with g? Color them green.

Skills: Recognition of the "g" sound; Sound/symbol association

The "k" sound

Kk

Which ones begin with k? Color them yellow.

Skills: Recognition of the "k" sound; Sound/symbol association

Beginning Phonics

The "m" sound

Which ones begin with m? Color them brown.

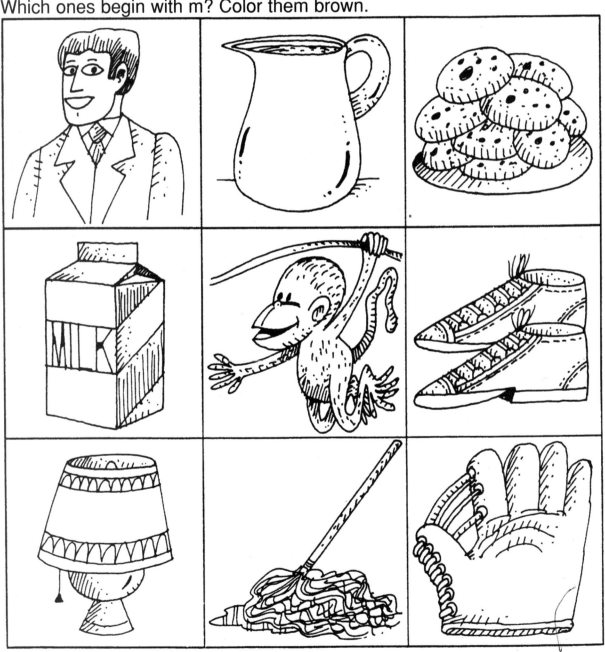

Skills: Recognition of the "m" sound; Sound/symbol association

The "p" sound

Which ones begin with p? Color them purple.

Skills: Recognition of the "p" sound; Sound/symbol association

The "v" sound

Which ones begin with v? Color them orange.

Skills: Recognition of the "v" sound; Sound/symbol association

The "r" sound

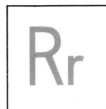

Which ones begin with r? Color them red.

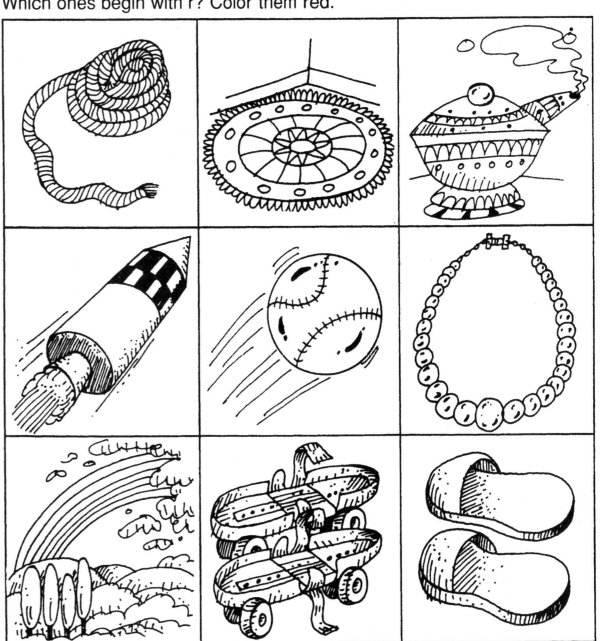

Skills: Recognition of the "r" sound; Sound/symbol association

The "s" sound

Which ones begin with s? Color them yellow.

Skills: Recognition of the "s" sound; Sound/symbol association

The "t" sound

Which ones begin with t? Color them orange.

Skills: Recognition of the "t" sound; Sound/symbol association

The "w" sound

W w

Which ones begin with w? Color them blue.

The "y" sound

Which ones begin with y? Color them green.

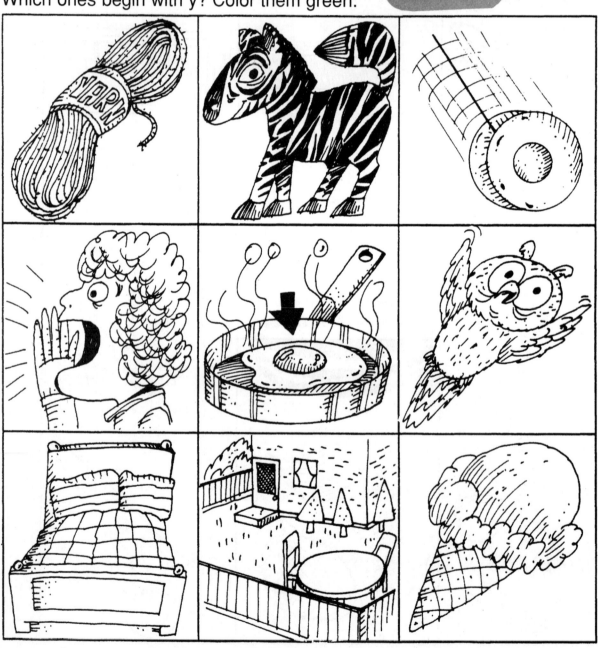

Skills: Recognition of the "y" sound; Sound/symbol association

Beginning Phonics

The "z" sound

Zz

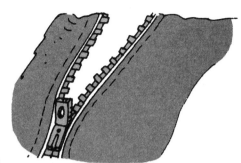

Which ones begin with z? Color them green.

Skills: Recognition of the "z" sound; Sound/symbol association

133

The "b" sound

Which ones begin with b? Say each "b" word out loud.

Skills: Auditory discrimination; Recognition of the "b" sound; Sound/symbol association

The "c" sound

Which ones begin with c? Say each "c" word out loud.

Skills: Auditory discrimination; Recognition of the "c" sound; Sound/symbol association

The "d" sound

Which ones begin with d? Say each "d" word out loud.

Skills: Auditory discrimination; Recognition of the "d" sound; Sound/symbol association

The "h" sound

Hh

Which ones begin with h? Say each "h" word out loud.

The "j" sound

Which ones begin with j? Say each "j" word out loud.

The "k" sound

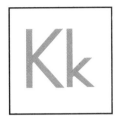

Which ones begin with k? Say each "k" word out loud.

Skills: Auditory discrimination; Recognition of the "k" sound; Sound/symbol association

The "l" sound

LI

Which ones begin with l? Say each "l" word out loud.

Skills: Auditory discrimination; Recognition of the "l" sound; Sound/symbol association

The "n" sound

Which ones begin with n? Say each "n" word out loud.

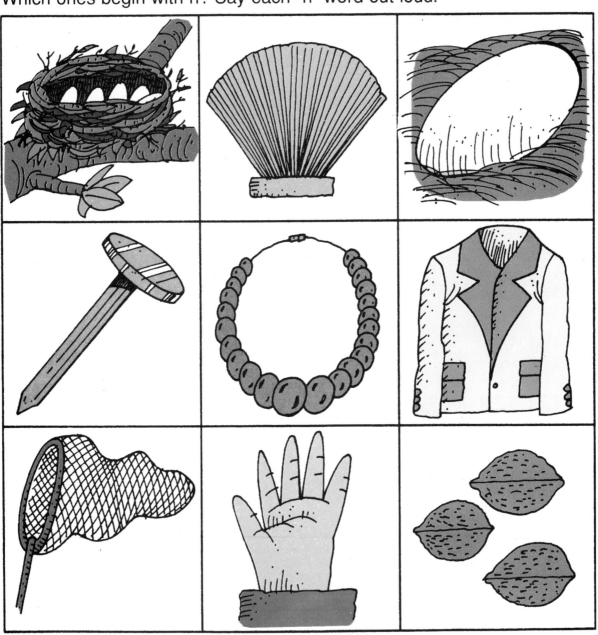

Skills: Auditory discrimination; Recognition of the "n" sound; Sound/symbol association

Beginning Phonics

The "q" sound

Q q	

Which ones begin with q? Say each "q" word out loud.

Skills: Auditory discrimination; Recognition of the "q" sound; Sound/symbol association

142

The "r" sound

Rr

Which ones begin with r? Say each "r" word out loud.

Skills: Auditory discrimination; Recognition of the "r" sound; Sound/symbol association

The "s" sound

Ss

Which ones begin with s? Say each "s" word out loud.

The "t" sound

Tt

Which ones begin with t? Say each "t" word out loud.

Skills: Auditory discrimination; Recognition of the "t" sound; Sound/symbol association

The "v" sound

Which ones begin with v? Say each "v" word out loud.

Skills: Auditory discrimination; Recognition of the "v" sound; Sound/symbol association

The "y" sound

Which ones begin with y? Say each "y" word out loud.

Skills: Auditory discrimination; Recognition of the "y" sound; Sound/symbol association

Say the name of each picture. Listen to the first sound.
Then circle the letters that make that sound.

Bb Mm Zz	Ff Bb Qq	Mm Gg Hh
Zz Tt Ff	Jj Pp Vv	Ss Yy Nn
Gg Rr Ll	Cc Yy Ww	Qq Ww Hh

Skills: Auditory and visual discrimination; Recognition of sounds and their symbols

Beginning Phonics

Say the name of each picture. Listen to the first sound.
Then circle the letters that make that sound.

Kk Mm Hh	Ff Dd Ww	Rr Gg Ff
Ss Tt Vv	Jj Pp Dd	Hh Ss Nn
Cc Rr Nn	Ss Ll Ww	Qq Ww Tt

Skills: Auditory and visual discrimination; Recognition of sounds and their symbols

Beginning Phonics

Say the name of each picture. Listen to the first sound.
Then circle the letters that make that sound.

Mm Kk Hh	Bb Ss Ff	Gg Hh Ww
Rr Nn Cc	Ll Pp Hh	Ss Mm Nn
Kk Rr Ll	Dd Yy Vv	Bb Ww Ff

Beginning Phonics

Look at the letters in each row.
Circle the picture whose name begins with the sound that letter makes.

Skills: Recognition of sounds and their symbols

151

Beginning Phonics

Look at the letters in each row.
Circle the picture whose name begins with the sound that letter makes.

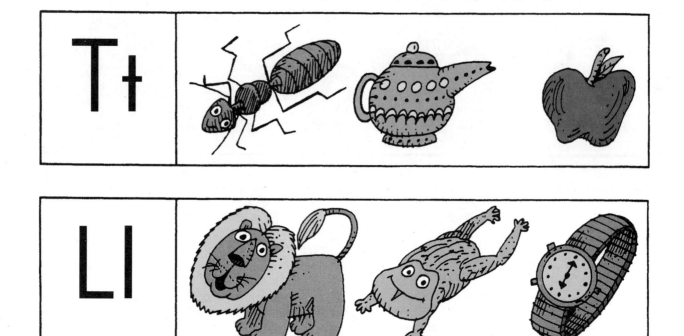

Beginning Phonics

Look at the letters in each row.
Circle the picture whose name begins with the sound that letter makes.

Beginning Phonics

Look at the letters in each row.
Circle the picture whose name begins with the sound that letter makes.

Skills: Recognition of sounds and their symbols

Beginning Phonics

Say the name of each picture.
Draw a line from each letter to the picture whose name ends with that sound.

b g m d t

Skills: Recognition of sounds and their symbols

Beginning Phonics

Look at the letter in each row.
Circle the picture whose name ends with that sound.

Skills: Recognition of sounds and their symbols

Beginning Phonics

Look at the letter in each row.
Circle the picture whose name ends with that sound.

k

m

l

n

Beginning Phonics

Look at the letter in each row.
Circle the picture whose name ends with that sound.

p

r

t

x

Skills: Recognition of sounds and their symbols

Final consonant: b

crib

Say the name of each picture.
Draw a line from the letter b
to each picture whose name
ends with the "b" sound.

Skills: Recognition of the final consonant "b" sound; Sound/symbol association

Final consonant: f

leaf

Say the name of each picture.
Draw a line from the letter f
to each picture whose name
ends with the "f" sound.

f

Skills: Recognition of the final consonant "f" sound; Sound/symbol association

Final consonant: d

sled

Say the name of each picture.
Draw a line from the letter d
to each picture whose name
ends with the "d" sound.

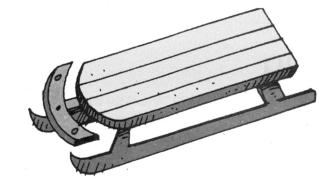

d

Skills: Recognition of the final consonant "d" sound; Sound/symbol association

Final consonant: g

bag

Say the name of each picture.
Draw a line from the letter g
to each picture whose name
ends with the "g" sound.

g

Final consonant: k

hook

Say the name of each picture. Draw a line from the letter k to each picture whose name ends with the "k" sound.

k

Skills: Recognition of the final consonant "k" sound; Sound/symbol association

Final consonant: m

broom

Say the name of each picture.
Draw a line from the letter m
to each picture whose name
ends with the "m" sound.

Skills: Recognition of the final consonant "m" sound; Sound/symbol association

Final consonant: l

sail

Say the name of each picture. Draw a line from the letter l to each picture whose name ends with the "l" sound.

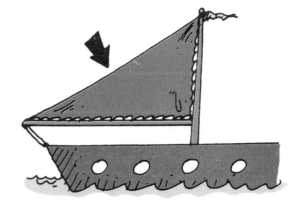

Skills: Recognition of the final consonant "l" sound; Sound/symbol association

Final consonant: n

chain

Say the name of each picture.
Draw a line from the letter n
to each picture whose name
ends with the "n" sound.

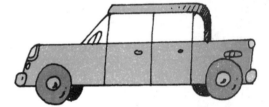

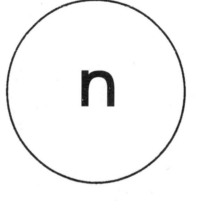

n

Skills: Recognition of the final consonant "n" sound; Sound/symbol association

Final consonant: p

top

Say the name of each picture.
Draw a line from the letter p
to each picture whose name
ends with the "p" sound.

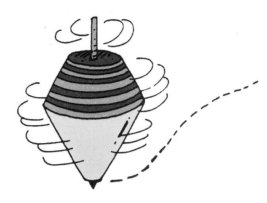

p

Final consonant: r

deer

Say the name of each picture.
Draw a line from the letter r
to each picture whose name
ends with the "r" sound.

r

Skills: Recognition of the final consonant "r" sound; Sound/symbol association

Final consonant: t

cat

Say the name of each picture.
Draw a line from the letter t
to each picture whose name
ends with the "t" sound.

Skills: Recognition of the final consonant "t" sound; Sound/symbol association

Final consonant: x

six

Say the name of each picture.
Draw a line from the letter x
to each picture whose name
ends with the "x" sound.

Skills: Recognition of the final consonant "x" sound; Sound/symbol association

Well Done!

Give yourself a star!

Words That Rhyme

Words That Rhyme

The word spot is part of the **ot** family.
Name these other things in the **ot** family.

cot

pot

hot

Skills: Recognizing words in the "ot" family

Words That Rhyme

The word bat is part of the **at** family.
Name these other things in the **at** family.

cat

hat

mat

Skills: Recognizing words in the "at" family

Words That Rhyme

The word bug is part of the **ug** family.
Name these other things in the **ug** family.

mug

jug

rug

Skills: Recognizing words in the "ug" family

176

The word cake is part of the **ake** family.
Name these other things in the **ake** family.

snake

rake

lake

Words That Rhyme

The word clown is part of the **own** family.
Name these other things in the **own** family.

crown

frown

down

Skills: Recognizing words in the "own" family

178

Words That Rhyme

The word swing is part of the **ing** family.
Name these other things in the **ing** family.

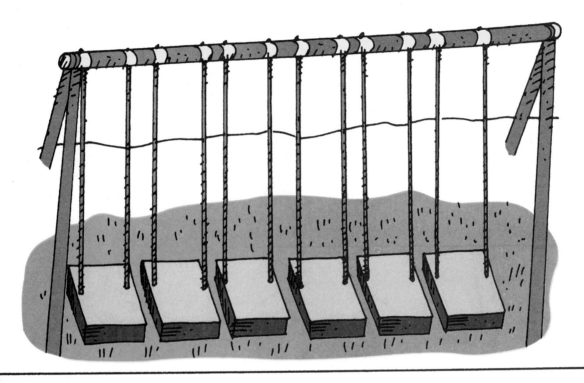

wing

ring

king

Skills: Recognizing words in the "ing" family

Words That Rhyme

Look at the picture of the cat. Say the name of each picture.
Draw a line from the cat to each picture whose name rhymes with the word **cat.**

Words That Rhyme

Look at the picture of the train. Say the name of each picture.
Draw a line from the train to each picture whose name rhymes with the word **train**.

Words That Rhyme

Look at the first picture in each row and say its name.
Circle the picture whose name rhymes with it.

Skills: Recognizing rhyming words

Words That Rhyme

Look at the first picture in each row and say its name.
Circle the picture whose name rhymes with it.

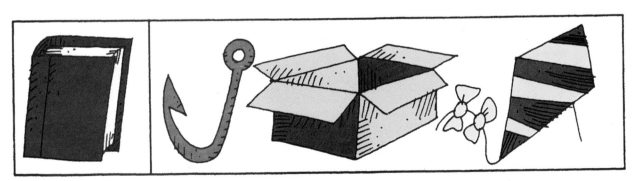

Skills: Recognizing rhyming words

Words That Rhyme

Look at the first picture in each row and say its name.
Circle the picture whose name rhymes with it.

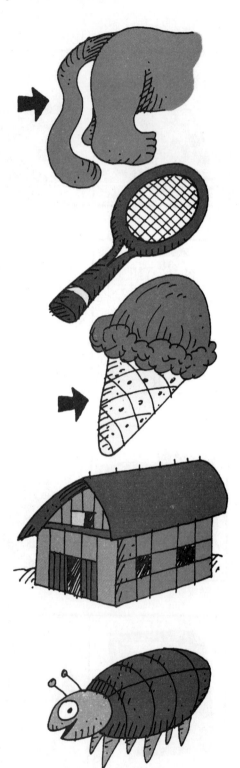

Skills: Recognizing rhyming words

Words That Rhyme

Look at each picture and say its name.
Draw a line to match each rhyming picture.

Skills: Recognizing rhyming words

Words That Rhyme

Look at each picture and say its name.
Draw a line to match each rhyming picture.

Skills: Recognizing rhyming words

Good Job!

Give yourself a star!

Colors and Shapes

red

Color these things that are red.

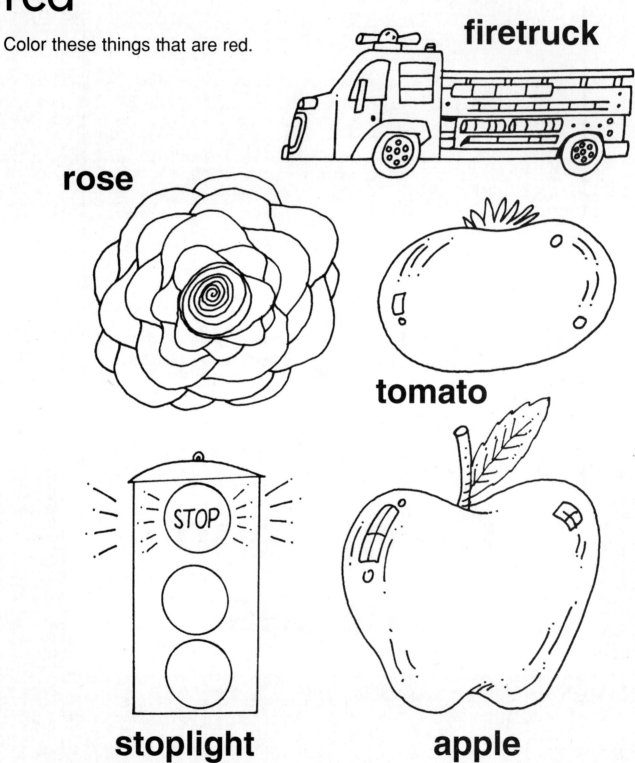

firetruck

rose

tomato

stoplight

STOP

apple

Skills: Distinguishing color; Classification; Word recognition

yellow

Color these things that are yellow.

corn

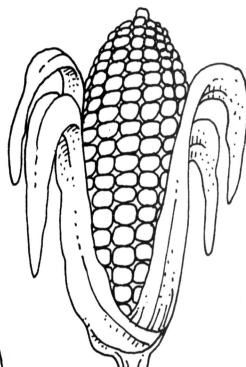

lemon

banana

chick

blue

Color these things that are blue.

blueberries

bluejay

mailbox

blue crayon

Skills: Distinguishing color; Classification; Word recognition

orange

Color these things that are orange.

oranges

pumpkin

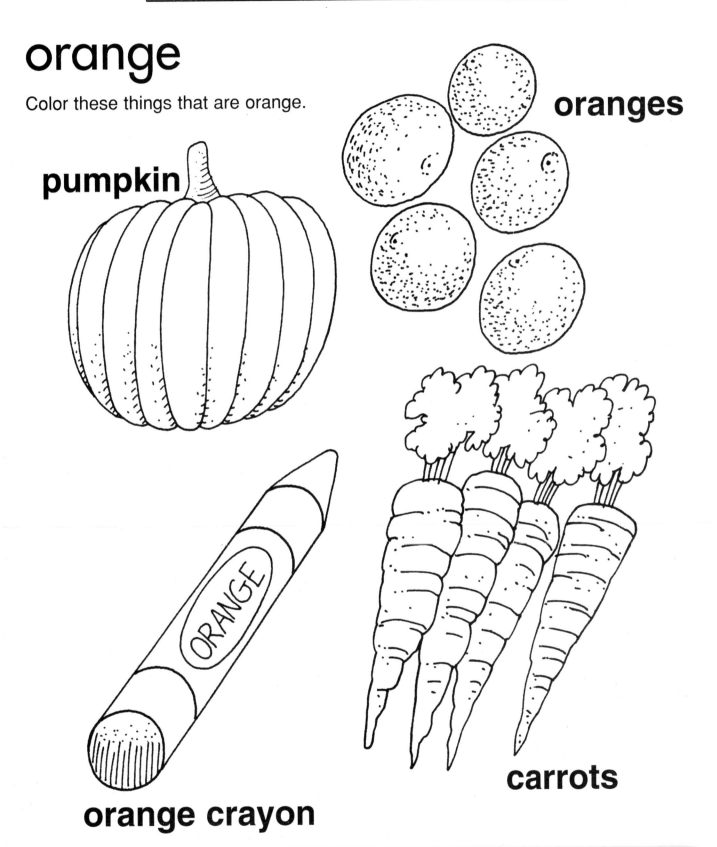

orange crayon

carrots

Skills: Distinguishing color; Classification; Word recognition

purple

Color these things that are purple.

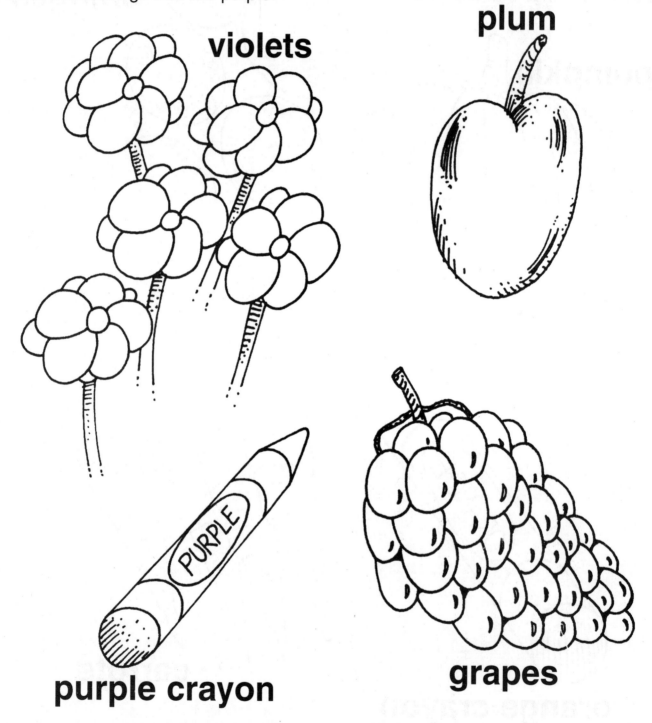

violets

plum

purple crayon

grapes

Skills: Distinguishing color; Classification; Word recognition

green

Color these things that are green.

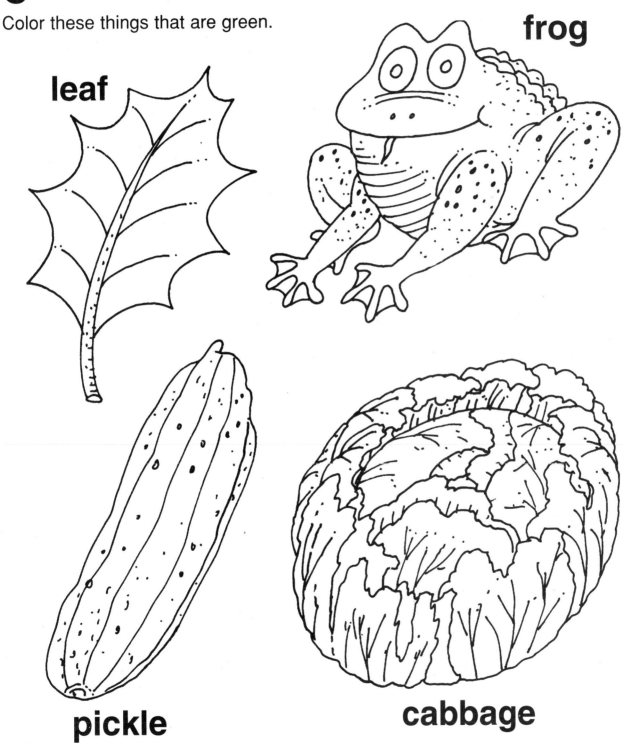

leaf

frog

pickle

cabbage

Skills: Distinguishing color; Classification; Word recognition

black

Color these things that are black.

witch's hat

black cat

seal

penguin

brown

Color these things that are brown.

potatoes

deer

logs

monkey

Skills: Distinguishing color; Classification; Word recognition

Look at the balloons.
Color each balloon to match the color word.
Then color the clown.

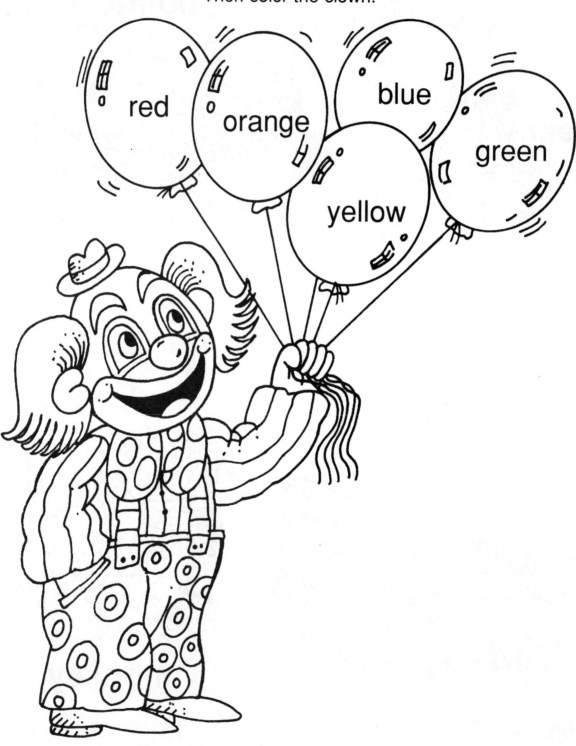

Skills: Distinguishing color; Visual memory of sight vocabulary

Look at the fish swimming in the ocean.
Color them to match the color words.
Then color the ocean blue.

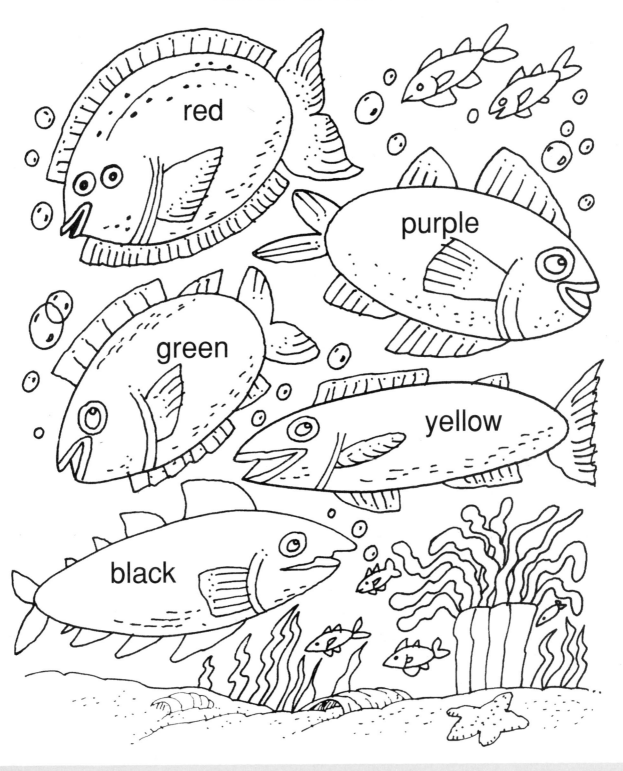

Skills: Distinguishing color; Visual memory of sight vocabulary

Colors and Shapes

Color each picture to match the color word.
Then look at the color word in each box.
Draw something that is that color.

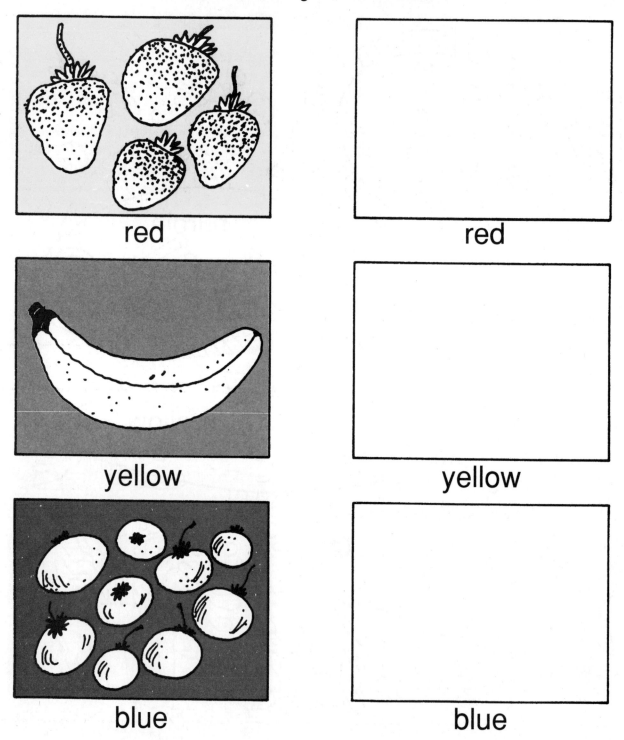

red

red

yellow

yellow

blue

blue

Skills: Following directions; Matching colors to color words; Responding creatively

Colors and Shapes

Trace the rectangles.
Then draw your own rectangles.
Color the shapes.

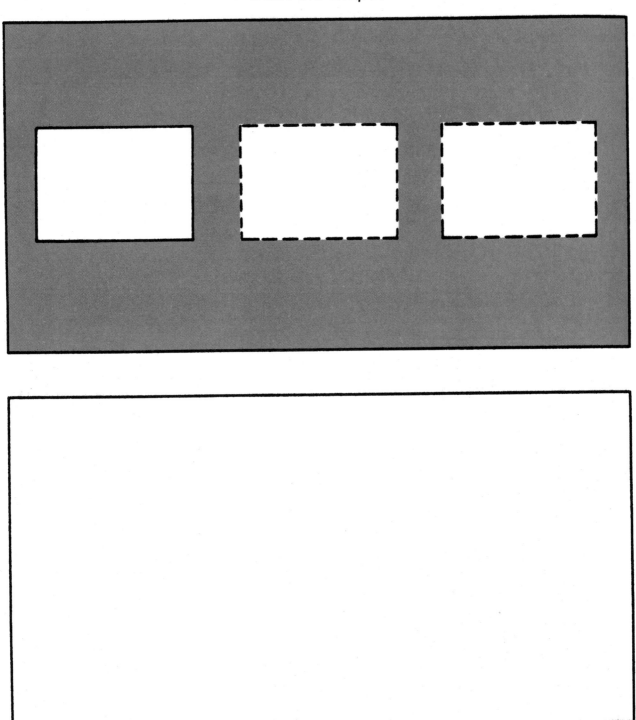

Skills: Fine motor skill development; Shape recognition

Colors and Shapes

Look at the rectangles at the top of the page.
Circle the objects that are shaped like rectangles.

Skills: Shape recognition; Visual discrimination; Recognizing shapes in objects

Trace the squares.
Then draw your own squares.
Color the shapes.

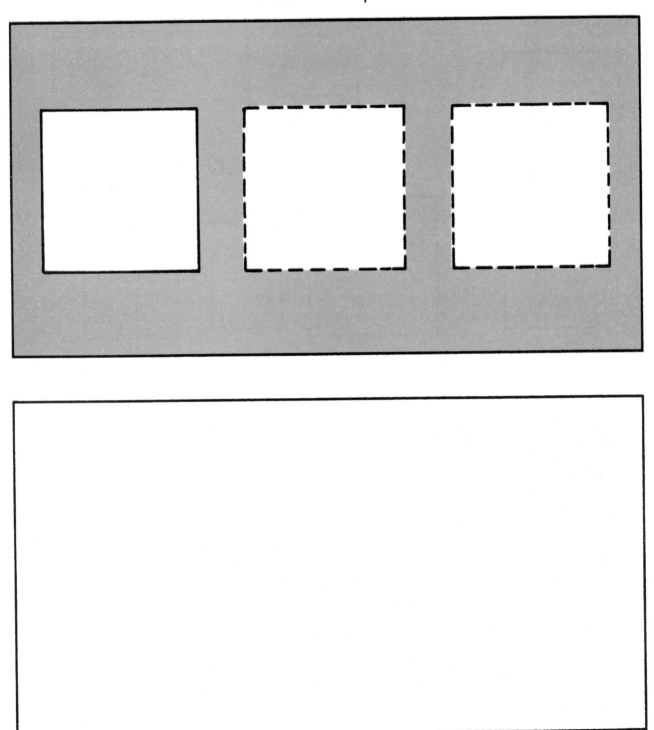

Skills: Fine motor skill development; Shape recognition

Colors and Shapes

Look at the squares at the top of the page.
Circle the objects that are shaped like squares.

Skills: Shape recognition; Visual discrimination; Recognizing shapes in objects

Colors and Shapes

Trace the triangles.
Then draw your own triangles.
Color the shapes.

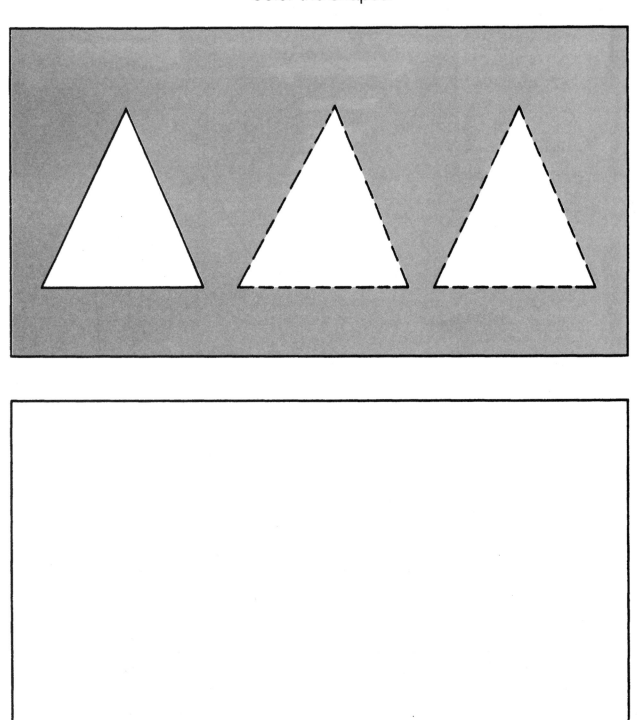

Skills: Fine motor skill development; Shape recognition

Colors and Shapes

Look at the triangles at the top of the page.
Circle the objects that are shaped like triangles.

Skills: Shape recognition; Visual discrimination; Recognizing shapes in objects

Colors and Shapes

Trace the circles.
Then draw your own circles.
Color the shapes.

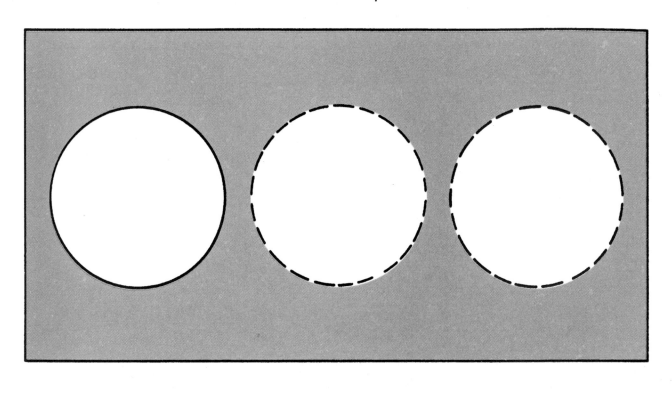

Skills: Fine motor skill development; Shape recognition

Colors and Shapes

Look at the circles at the top of the page.
Circle the objects that are shaped like circles.

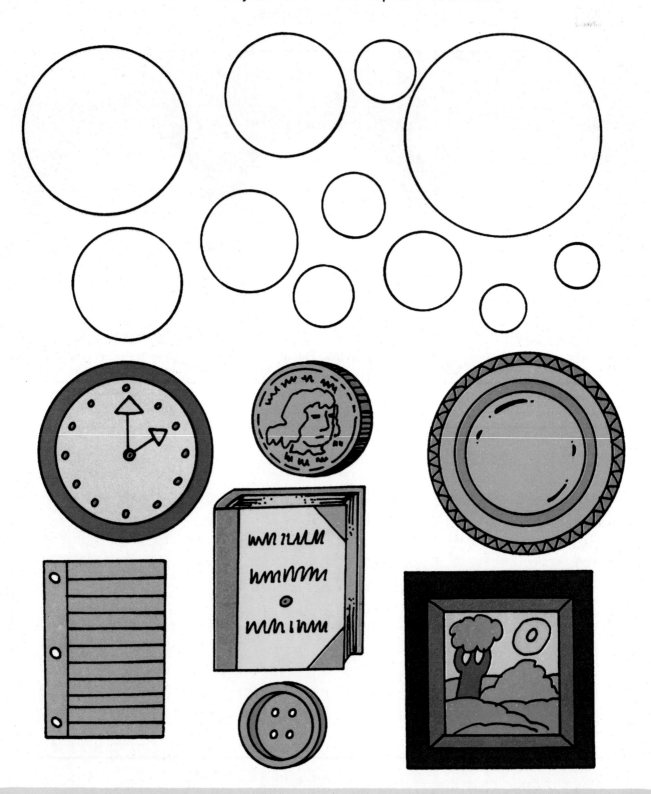

Skills: Shape recognition; Visual discrimination; Recognizing shapes in objects

Colors and Shapes

Look at the circle. Look at the rectangle.
Color the circles yellow.
Color the rectangles green.

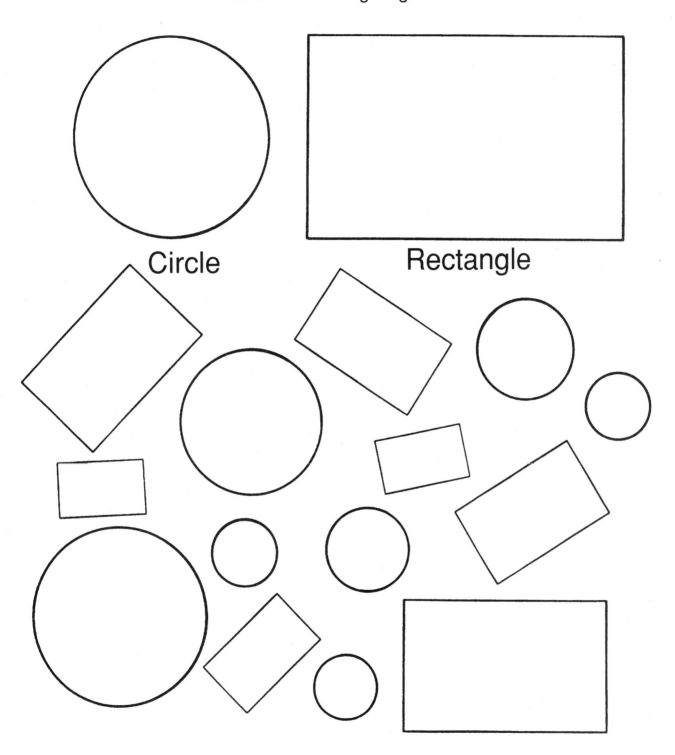

Circle   Rectangle

Skills: Shape recognition; Visual discrimination; Color recognition

Colors and Shapes

Look at the triangle. Look at the square.
Color the triangles red.
Color the squares blue.

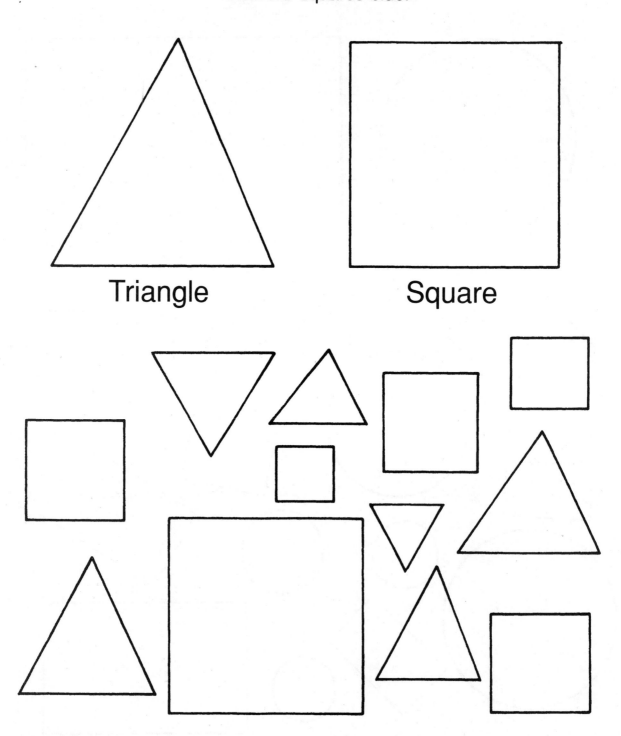

Triangle　　　　　Square

Skills: Shape recognition; Visual discrimination; Color recognition

Colors and Shapes

Color the squares red. Color the circles blue.
Color the triangles yellow. Color the rectangles green.

Skills: Shape recognition; Visual discrimination; Color recognition

Color the squares red. Color the circles blue.
Color the triangles yellow. Color the rectangles green.

Skills: Shape recognition; Visual discrimination; Color recognition

Colors and Shapes

Color these things that are red.

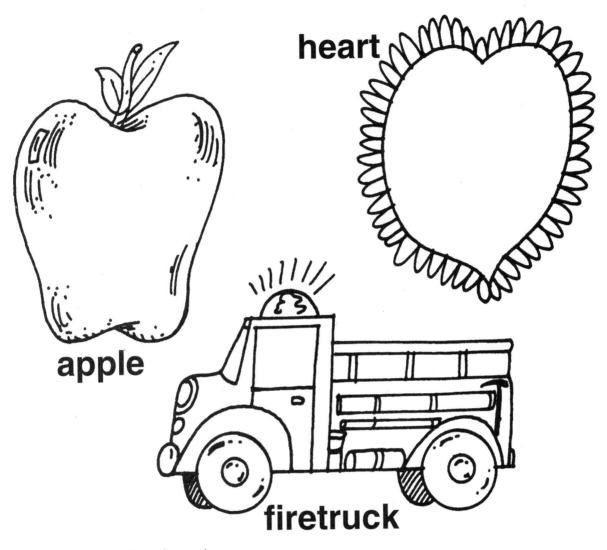

heart

apple

firetruck

Draw something that is red.

Skills: Distinguishing colors

213

Color these things that are purple.

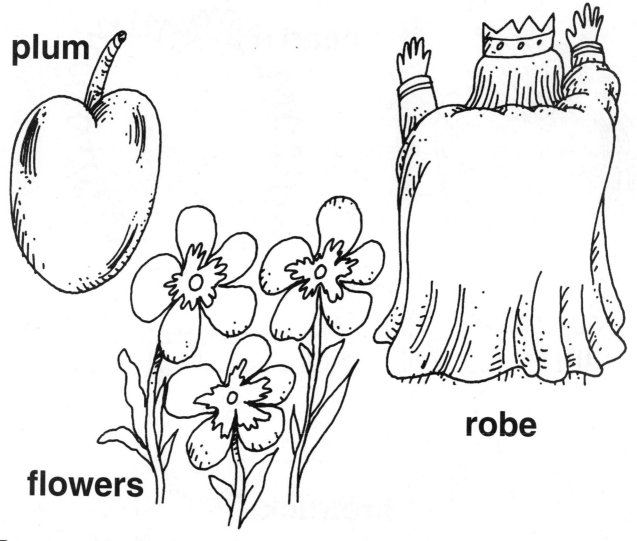

plum

flowers

robe

Draw something that is purple.

Skills: Distinguishing colors

Color these things that are green.

leaf

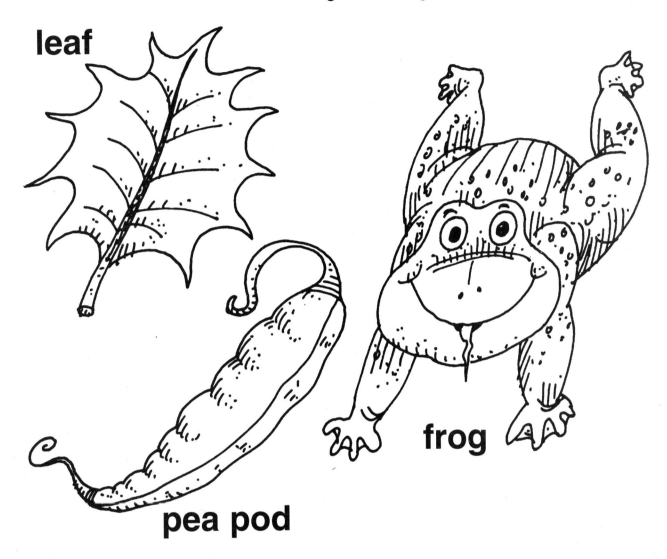

pea pod

frog

Draw something that is green.

Skills: Distinguishing colors

Color these things that are yellow.

corn

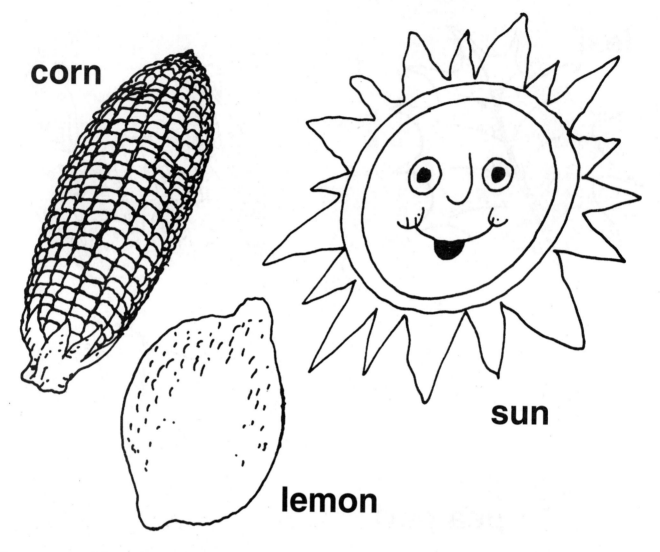

sun

lemon

Draw something that is yellow.

Skills: Distinguishing colors

Color these things that are orange.

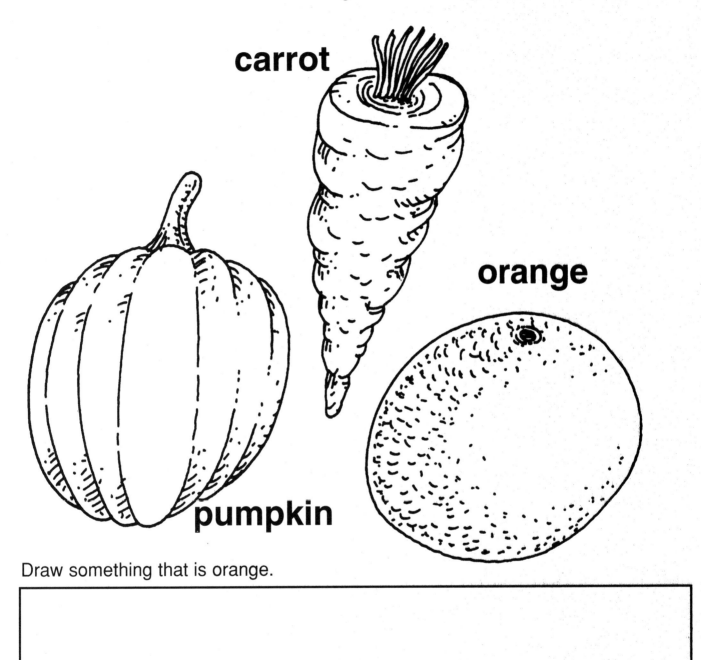

carrot

orange

pumpkin

Draw something that is orange.

Skills: Distinguishing colors

217

Color these things that are brown.

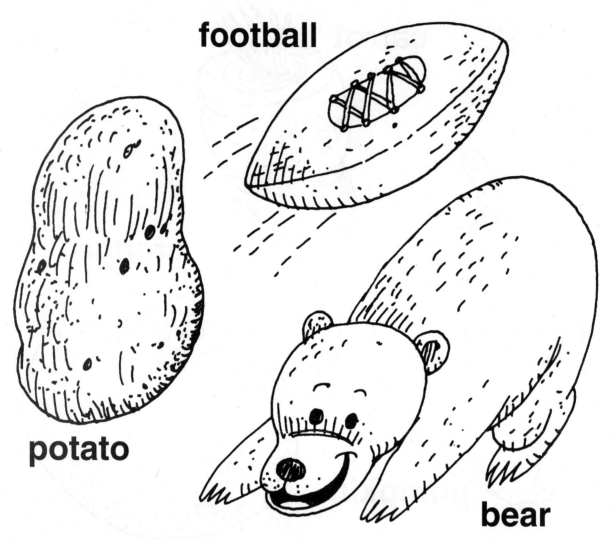

football

potato

bear

Draw something that is brown.

Skills: Distinguishing colors

Color these things that are black.

spider

witch's hat

bat

Draw something that is black.

Skills: Distinguishing colors

Colors and Shapes

Look at the birds in the park.
Color each bird to match the color word.

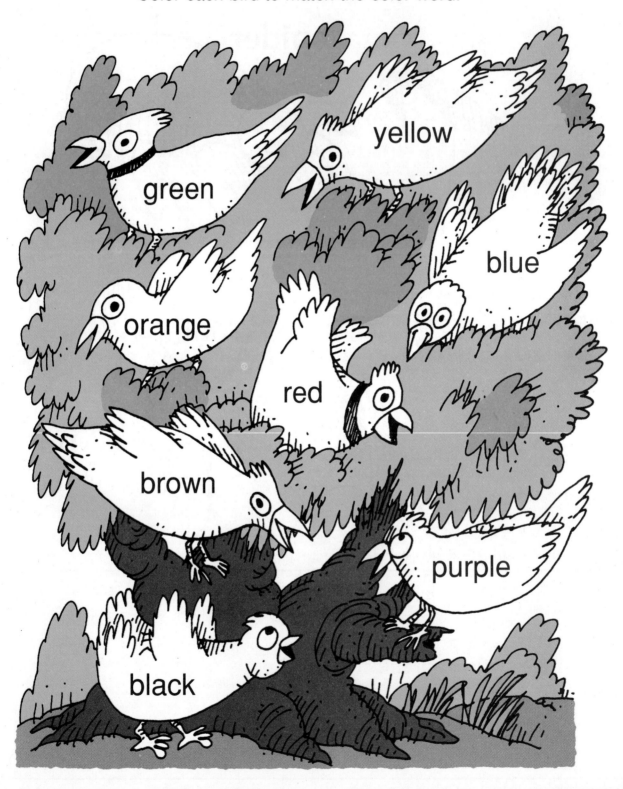

Skills: Distinguishing colors and color words

Excellent!

Give yourself a star!

Math Readiness Skills

Math Readiness Skills

Look at the picture in each box.
Circle the animal that is on the top.
Then color the pictures.

Skills: Recognizing position (top)

Math Readiness Skills

Look at the picture in each box.
Circle the child that is on the bottom.
Then color the pictures.

Skills: Recognizing position (bottom)

225

Math Readiness Skills

Look at the picture in each box.
Circle the animal that is in the middle.
Then color the pictures.

Skills: Recognizing position (middle)

226

Look at the picture in each box.
Circle the animal that is outside.
Then color the pictures.

Skills: Recognizing position (outside)

Look at the picture in each box.
Circle the object that is inside.
Then color the pictures.

Skills: Recognizing position (inside)

Math Readiness Skills

Look at the pattern in each row. Circle a picture at the end of each row that continues the pattern. Then color the pictures.

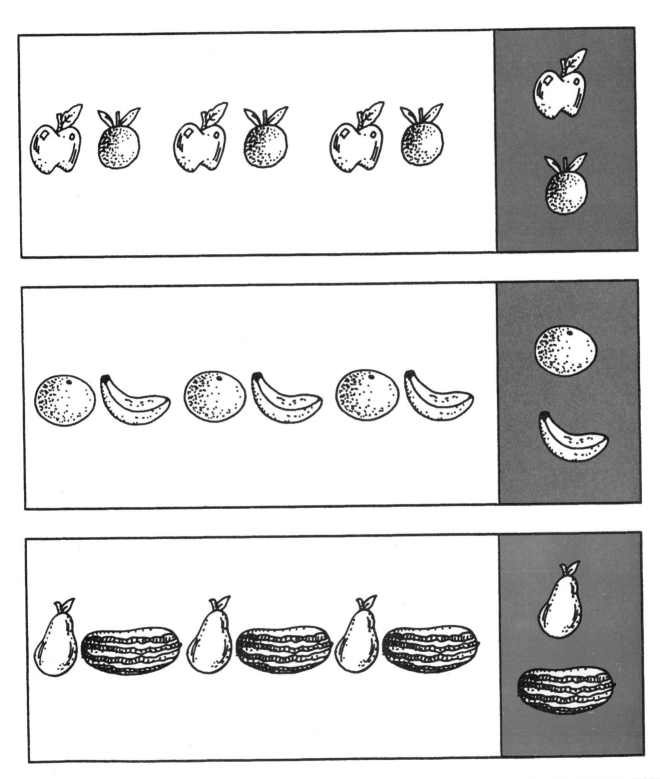

Look at the pattern in each row. Circle a picture at the end of each row that continues the pattern. Then color the pictures.

Skills: Observing and reproducing patterns; Visual memory; Fine motor skill development

Which one is large?
Look at the pictures in each row. Circle the one that is large.
Then color the pictures.

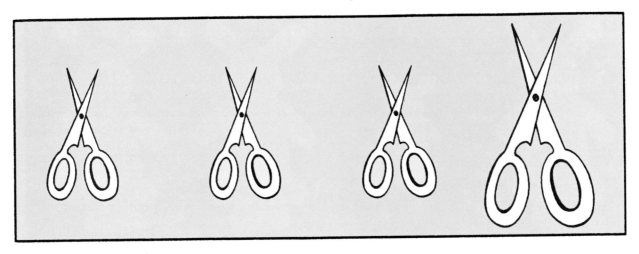

Skills: Visual discrimination; Making comparisons; Following directions

Math Readiness Skills

Which one is small?
Look at the pictures in each row. Circle the one that is small.
Then color the pictures.

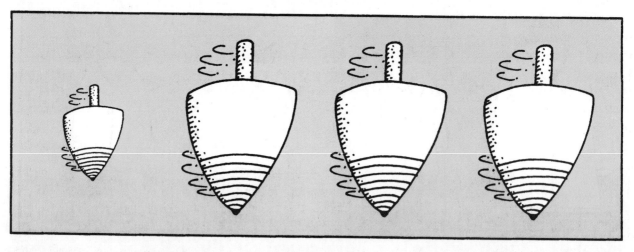

Skills: Visual discrimination; Making comparisons; Following directions

Math Readiness Skills

Look at the pictures in each box.
Color the small pictures green.
Color the large pictures yellow.

Skills: Making comparisons; Visual Discrimination

Look at the pictures in each box.
Circle the picture of the person who is shorter.
Then color the pictures.

Skills: Making comparisons; Visual discrimination

Math Readiness Skills

Look at the pictures in each box.
Circle the picture of the person who is taller.
Then color the pictures.

Skills: Making comparisons; Visual discrimination

Math Readiness Skills

Which one is shorter?
Look at the pictures in each box. Circle the one that is shorter.
Then color the pictures.

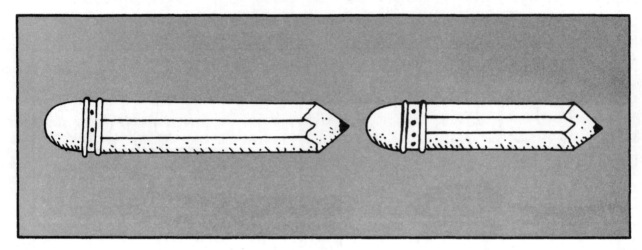

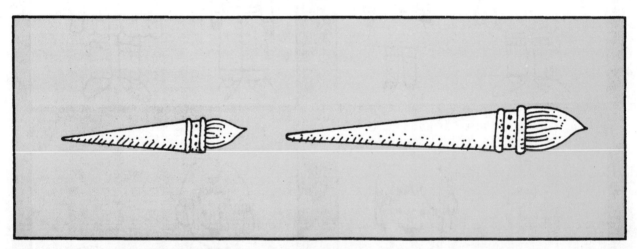

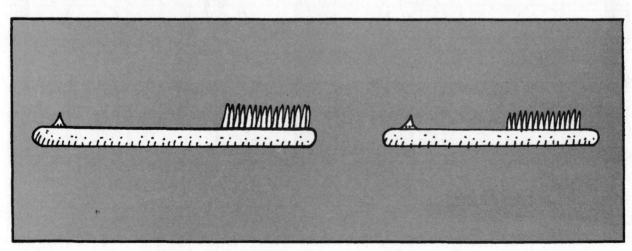

Skills: Making comparisons; Visual discrimination

Math Readiness Skills

Which one is longer?
Look at the pictures in each box. Circle the one that is longer.
Then color the pictures.

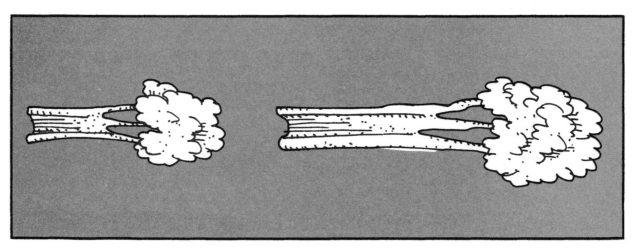

Math Readiness Skills

Look at the pictures in each box.
Draw lines to match each object on the top to an object on the bottom.
Then color the pictures.

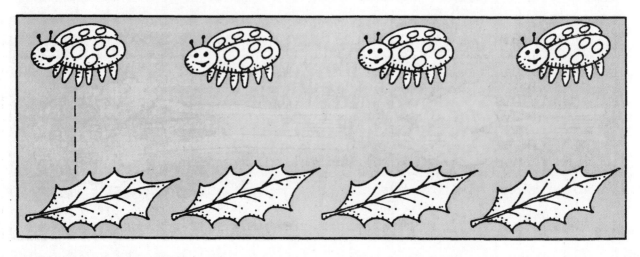

Skills: One-to-one correspondence; Association

238

Math Readiness Skills

Look at the pictures in each box.
Draw lines to match each object on one side to an object on the other side.
Then color the pictures.

Skills: One-to-one correspondence; Association

Math Readiness Skills

Look at the pictures in each box. Draw a ball for each animal.
Then color the pictures. The first one is done for you.

Skills: One-to-one correspondence; Development of number sense

240

Math Readiness Skills

Look at the pictures in each box.
Circle the group that shows less.
Then color the pictures.

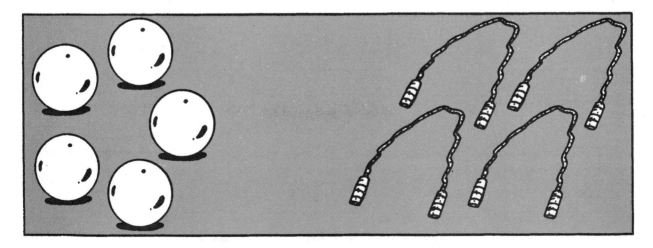

Math Readiness Skills

Look at the pictures in each box.
Circle the group that shows more.
Then color the pictures.

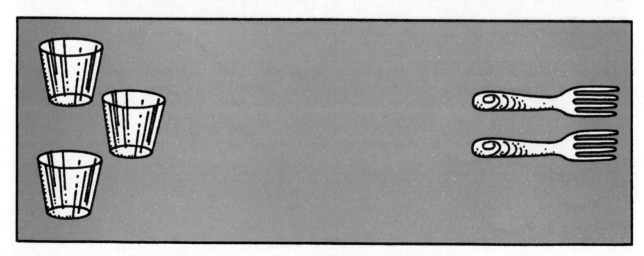

Skills: Making comparisons; Development of number sense

The turtle at the top of the page is facing right.
Circle the pictures that show turtles facing right.

Skills: Recognizing left and right; Position

Math Readiness Skills

The turkey at the top of the page is facing left.
Draw a line under the pictures that show turkeys facing left.

left

Skills: Recognizing left and right; Position

Math Readiness Skills

Look at the pictures at the top of the page.
One horse is facing left. One horse is facing right.
Circle the pictures that show animals facing left.
Draw a line under the pictures that show animals facing right.

left   right

Skills: Recognizing left and right; Position

Math Readiness Skills

Look at the hands at the top of the page.
One hand is on the left. One hand is on the right.
Circle the picture in each box that is on the left.
Draw a line under the picture in each box that is on the right.

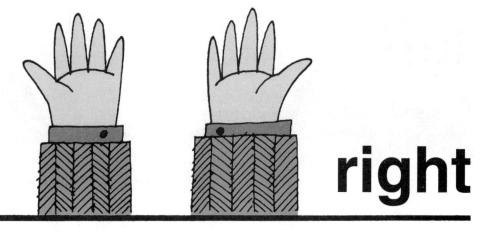

left   **right**

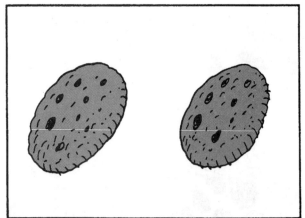

Skills: Recognizing left and right; Position

Look at the picture in each box.
Look at the word left or right under each picture.
Circle the object that is on the correct side.

left

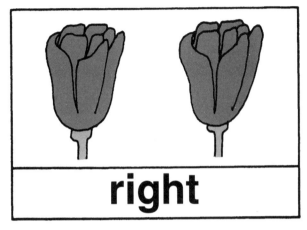

right

left

right

left

right

Skills: Recognizing left and right; Position

Math Readiness Skills

Look at the picture in each box.
Look at the word left or right under each picture.
Circle the object that is on the correct side.

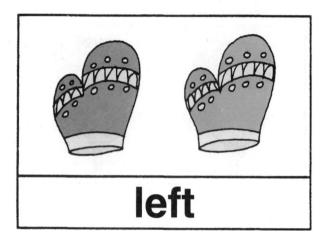

left

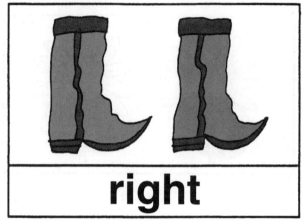

right

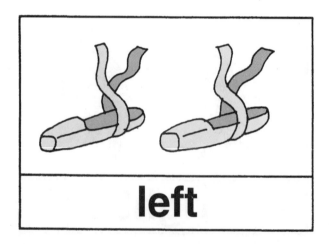

left

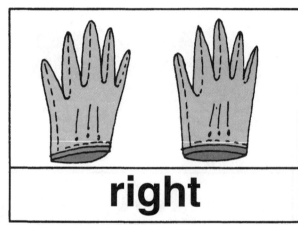

right

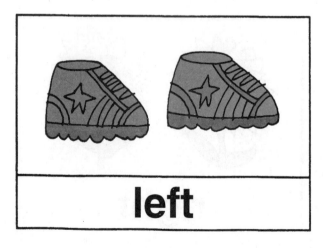

left

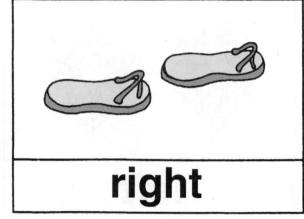

right

Skills: Recognizing left and right; Position

Math Readiness Skills

Look at the pictures in each row.
Circle the picture of the animal that is first in line.
Then color the pictures.

Skills: Recognizing ordinal numbers (first); Position

Math Readiness Skills

Look at the pictures in each row.
Circle the picture of the animal that is second in line.
Then color the pictures.

Skills: Recognizing ordinal numbers (second); Position

Math Readiness Skills

Look at the pictures in each row.
Circle the picture of the animal that is third in line.
Then color the pictures.

Skills: Recognizing ordinal numbers (third); Position

Math Readiness Skills

Look at the pictures in each row.
Circle the first picture in each row.
Draw a line under the second picture in each row.
Color the third picture in each row.

Well Done!

Give yourself a star!

Number Concepts

How many elephants do you see?
Trace the number.
Then color the picture.

Skills: Recognizing a set of "1"; Forming the numeral "1"

Look at the set in each box.
Circle the sets that show "1".
Then color the pictures.

Skills: Identifying sets of "1"

How many apes do you see?
Trace the number.
Then color the pictures.

Skills: Recognizing a set of "2"; Forming the numeral "2"

Number Concepts

Look at the number in the center of the page.
Find the sets that show "2".
Draw a line from those pictures to the number 2.

How many hippos do you see?
Trace the number.
Then color the pictures.

Number Concepts

Look at the pictures in each row.
Color three of each animal.

Skills: Creating sets of "3"

How many walruses do you see?
Trace the number.
Then color the pictures.

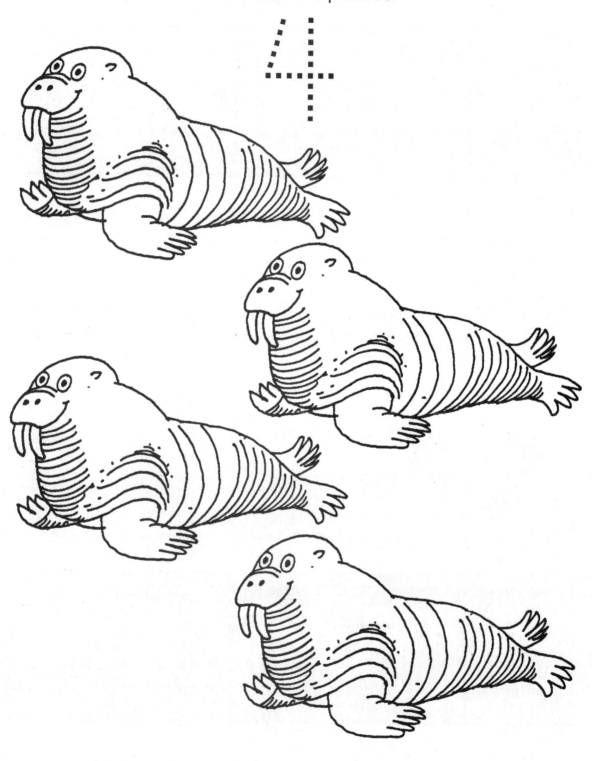

Skills: Recognizing a set of "4"; Forming the numeral "4"

262

Number Concepts

Look at the set in each box.
Circle the number that tells how many animals are in each set.
Then color the pictures.

3   4   5

2   3   4

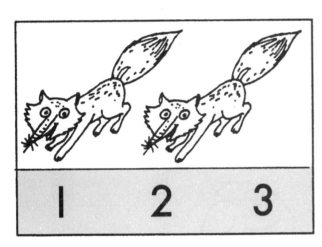

1   2   3

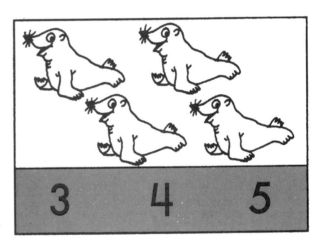

3   4   5

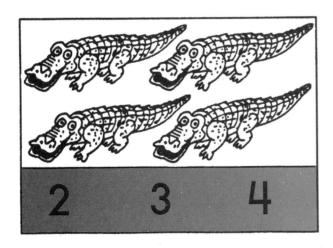

2   3   4

1   2   3

How many parrots do you see?
Trace the number.
Then color the pictures.

Look at the number at the beginning of each row.
Circle that number of animals.
Then color the pictures.

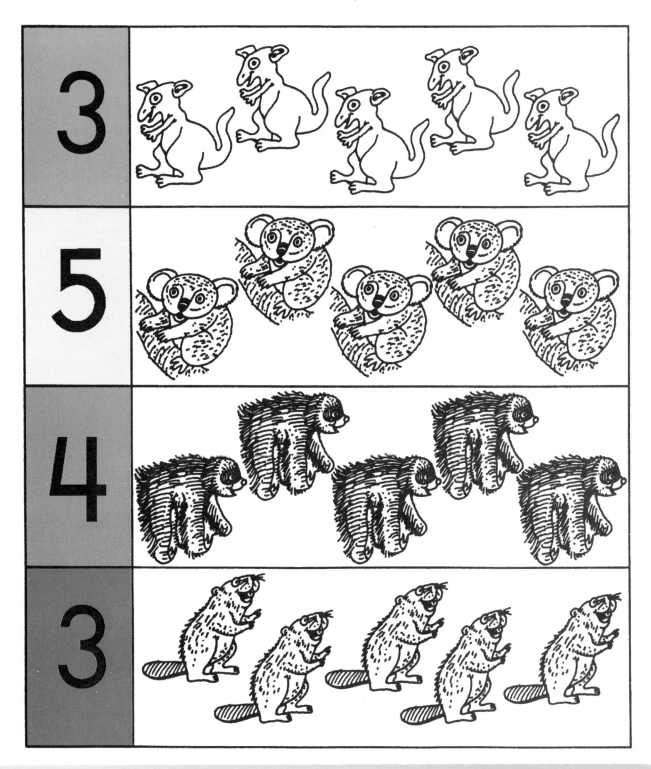

How many monkeys do you see?
Trace the number.
Then color the pictures.

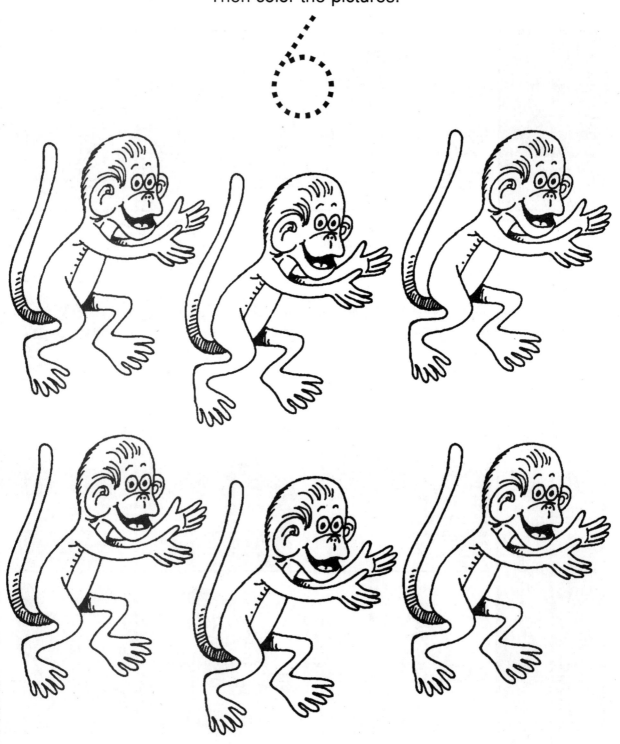

Skills: Recognizing a set of "6"; Forming the numeral "6"

Look at the sets in each box.
Circle the number that tells how many animals are in each set.
Then color the pictures.

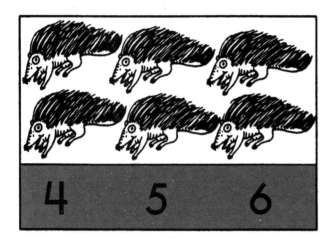

4   5   6

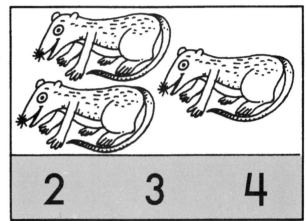

2   3   4

3   4   5

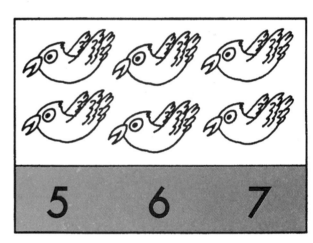

5   6   7

1   2   3

6   7   8

Skills: Identifying sets

How many birds do you see?
Trace the number.
Then color the pictures.

Number Concepts

Look at each set.
Color the sets that show "7".

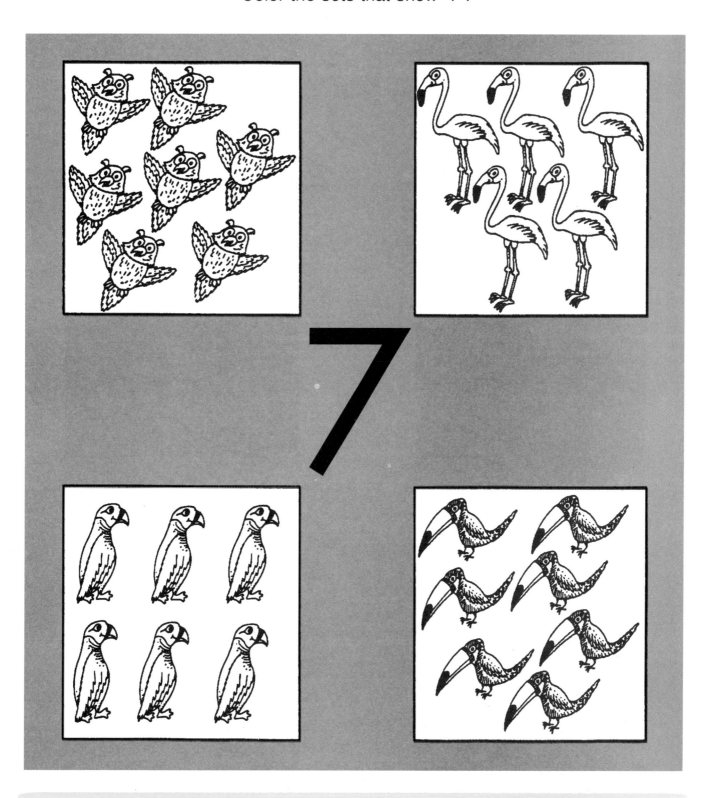

How many turtles do you see?
Trace the number.
Then color the pictures.

How many animals do you see in each big box?
Write the number in the small box.
Then color the sets that show "8".

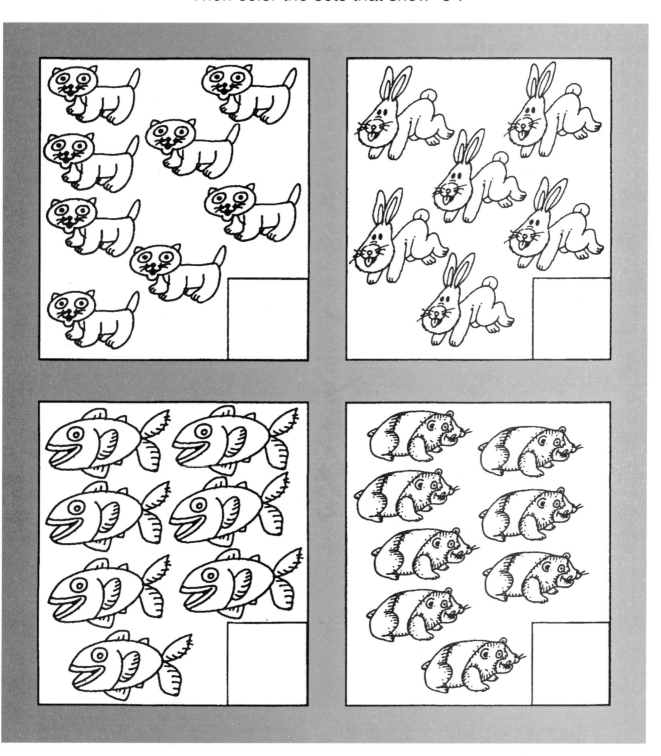

Skills: Identifying sets of "8"

How many porcupines do you see?
Trace the number.
Then color the pictures.

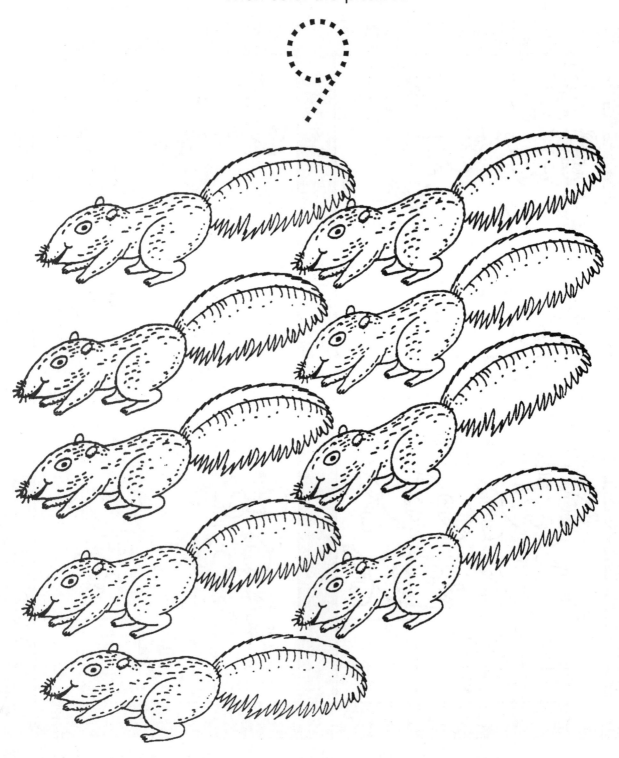

Skills: Recognizing a set of "9"; Forming the numeral "9"

Number Concepts

Look at the pictures in each box.
Color each row to show sets of "9".

How many dogs do you see?
Trace the number.
Then color the pictures.

Number Concepts

How many pictures do you see in each big box?
Write the number in the small box.
Then color the sets that show "10".

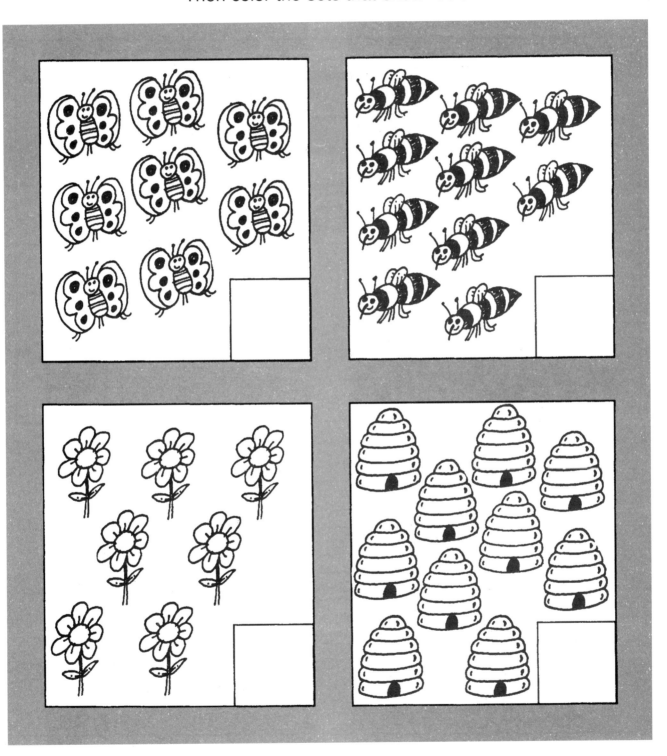

How many grasshoppers do you see?
Draw another set to show the same number.
Then trace and print the number and number word.

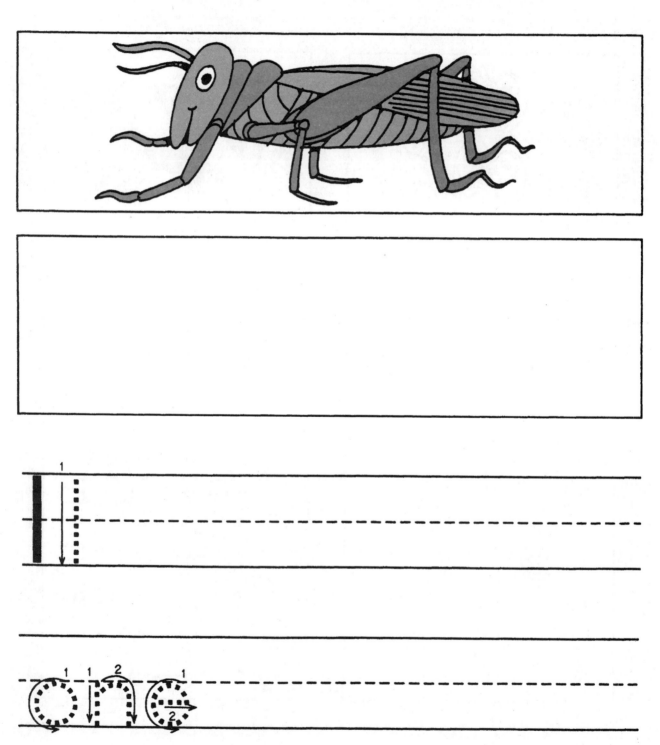

How many spiders do you see?
Draw another set to show the same number.
Then trace and print the number and number word.

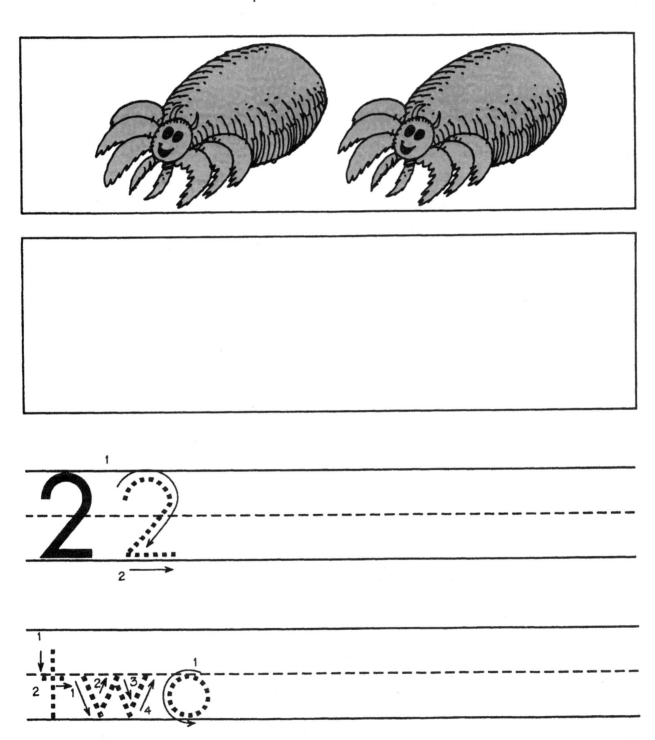

How many bees do you see?
Draw another set to show the same number.
Then trace and print the number and number word.

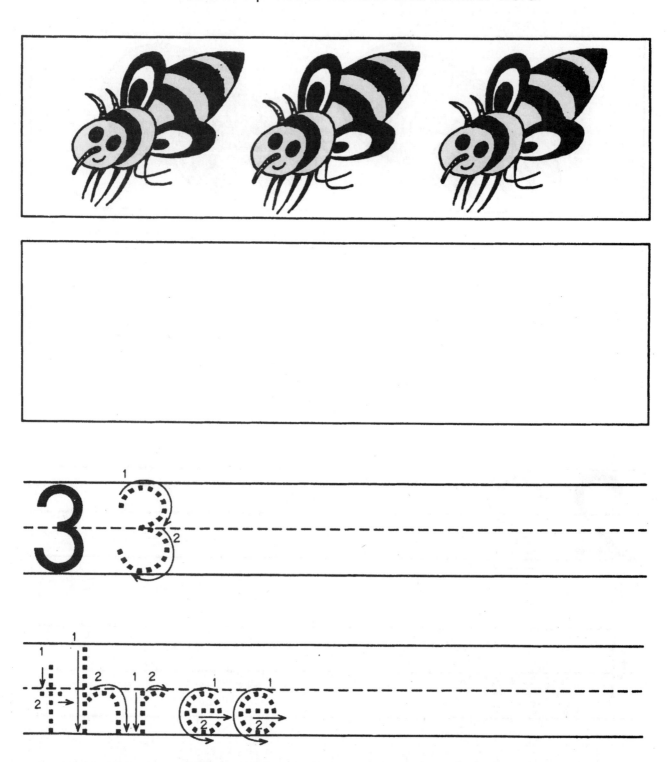

Number Concepts

How many ladybugs do you see?
Draw another set to show the same number.
Then trace and print the number and number word.

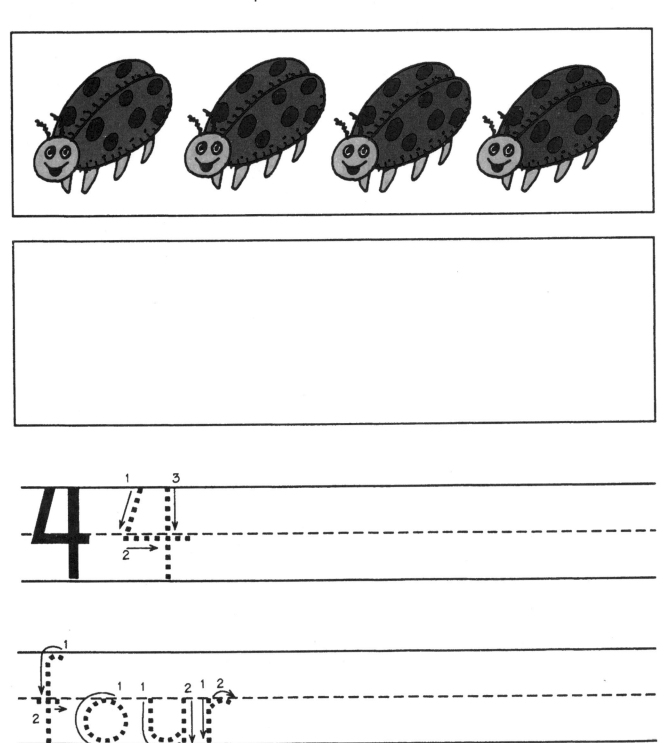

How many butterflies do you see?
Draw another set to show the same number.
Then trace and print the number and number word.

How many inch worms do you see?
Draw another set to show the same number.
Then trace and print the number and number word.

How many flies do you see?
Draw another set to show the same number.
Then trace and print the number and number word.

How many caterpillars do you see?
Draw another set to show the same number.
Then trace and print the number and number word.

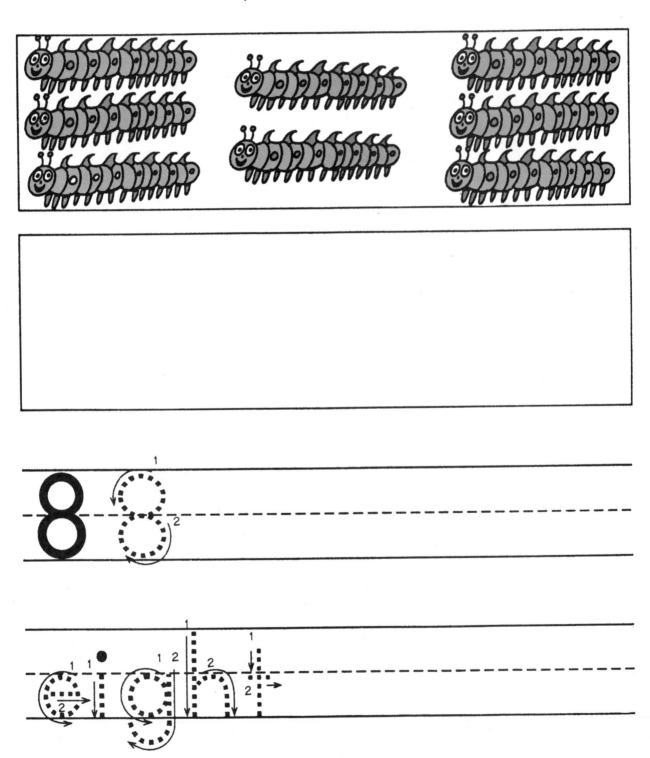

How many snails do you see?
Draw another set to show the same number.
Then trace and print the number and number word.

Number Concepts

How many fireflies do you see?
Draw another set to show the same number.
Then trace and print the number and number word.

Connect the dots from 1 to 10 to find out who is joining the picnic.

Skills: Number order; Recognition of numerals

Number Concepts

How many musical instruments are in each set?
Draw a line to match the sets with the same number of objects.

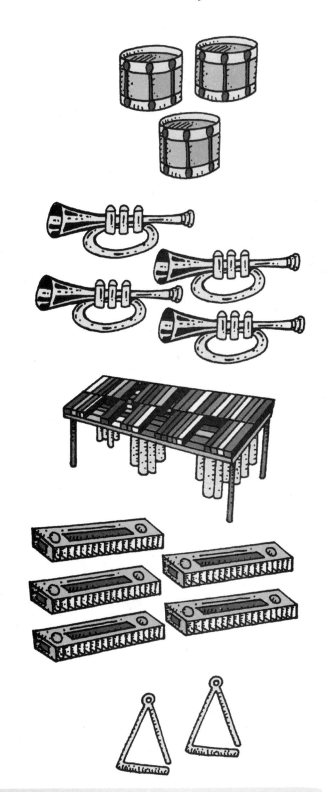

Number Concepts

How many sea creatures are in each set?
Draw a line to match the sets with the same number of creatures.

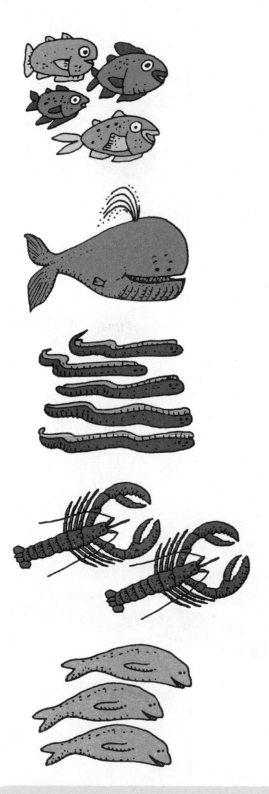

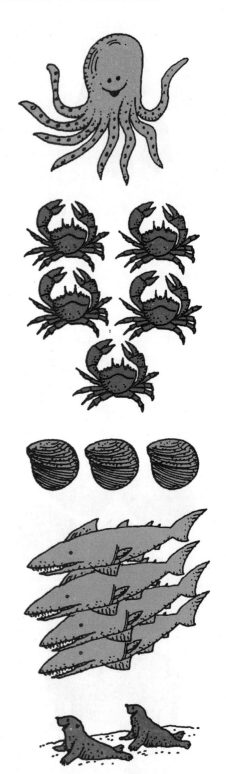

Number Concepts

Circle the number that tells how many pieces of fruit are in each box.
Then color the pictures.

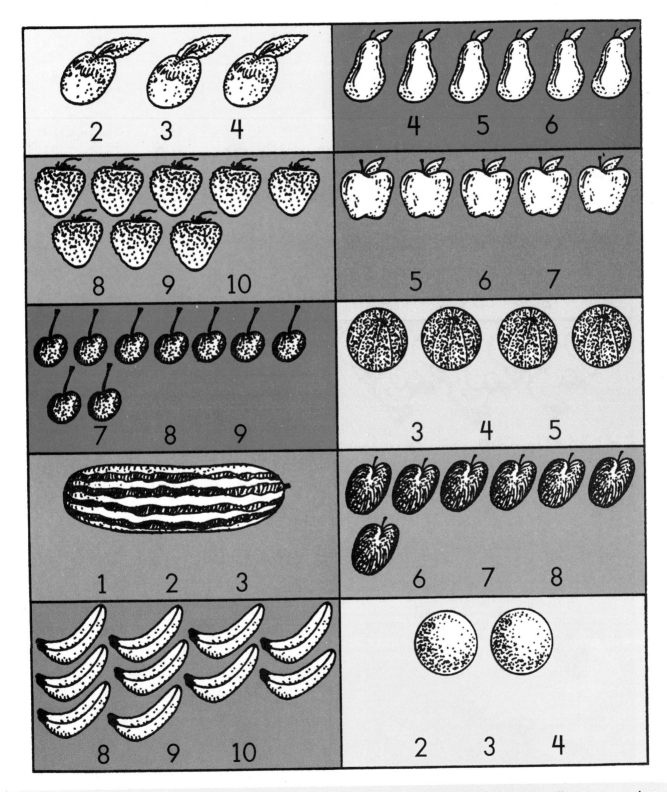

Circle the number that tells how many animals are in each box.
Then color the pictures.

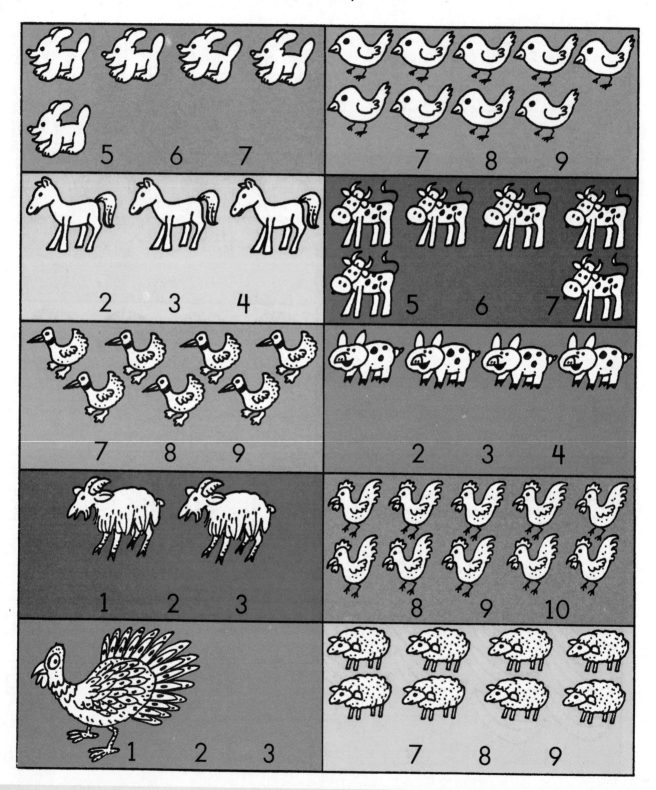

Number Concepts

Color the correct number of shapes.
The number at the beginning of each row tells how many.

1	○ ○ ○ ○ ○ ○ ○ ○ ○ ○
2	△ △ △ △ △ △ △ △ △ △
3	□ □ □ □ □ □ □ □ □ □
4	☆ ☆ ☆ ☆ ☆ ☆ ☆ ☆ ☆ ☆
5	▯ ▯ ▯ ▯ ▯ ▯ ▯ ▯ ▯ ▯

Skills: Creating sets of objects; Recognizing numerals

Number Concepts

Color the correct number of shapes.
The number at the beginning of each row tells how many.

6	○○○○○○○○○○
7	▢▢▢▢▢▢▢▢▢▢
8	○○○○○○○○○○
9	▢▢▢▢▢▢▢▢▢▢
10	△△△△△△△△△△

Skills: Creating sets of objects; Recognizing numerals

292

Practice Page

Use these pages to practice writing letters and numbers.

Practice Page

Good Job!

Give yourself a star!

Working with Numbers

Working with Numbers

Look at each box.
How many objects are in the group?
Write the number.

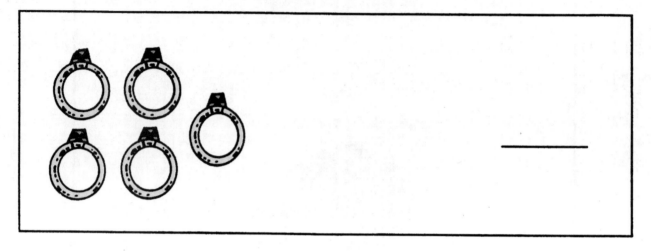

_____

_____

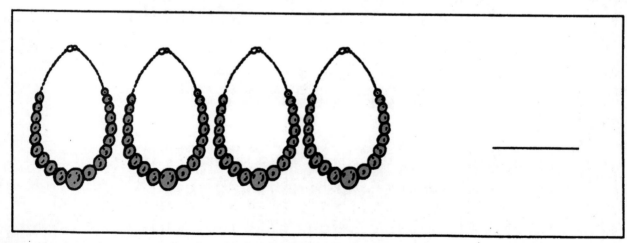

_____

Skills: Counting; Writing numerals

Working with Numbers

Look at each box.
How many objects are in the group?
Write the number.

_____

_____

_____

Skills: Counting; Writing numerals

Working with Numbers

Look at each box.
How many utensils are in the group?
Write the number.

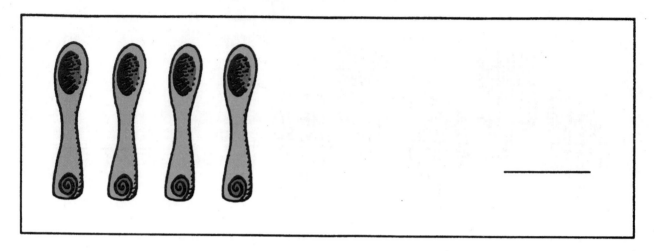

_____

_____

_____

Skills: Counting; Writing numerals

300

Working with Numbers

Look at each box.
How many objects are in the group?
Write the number.

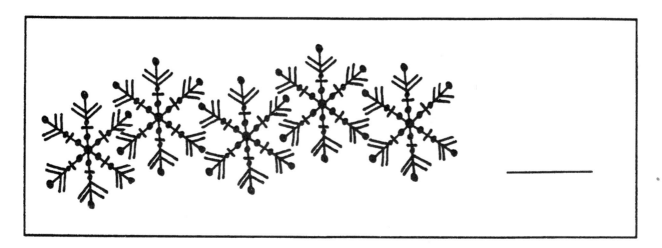

_____

_____

_____

Skills: Counting; Writing numerals

Look at each box.
How many objects are in the group?
Write the number.

_____

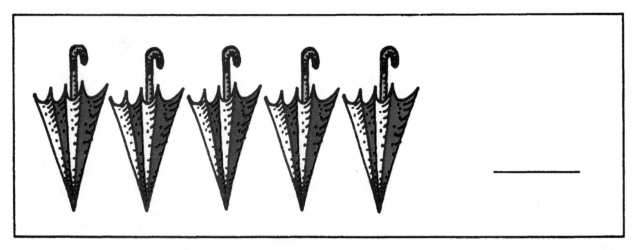

_____

_____

Skills: Counting; Writing numerals

Working with Numbers

How many pieces of fruit are in each group?
Circle the correct number.

4 5 6	3 4 5
4 5 6	3 4 5

Working with Numbers

How many objects are in each group?
Circle the correct number.

6
7
8

7
8
9

6
7
8

5
6
7

Working with Numbers

How many objects are in each group?
Circle the correct number.

4
5
6

6
7
8

7
8
9

6
7
8

Skills: Counting

305

Working with Numbers

Count the dolphins.
How many are in the top row? _____
How many are in the bottom row? _____
How many are there in all? _____
Write the numbers.

Working with Numbers

Look at the pictures in each box.
How many insects are there?
Write the number.

_____

_____

_____

Skills: Counting; Writing numerals

Working with Numbers

Look at the pictures in each box.
How many insects are there?
Write the number.

_____

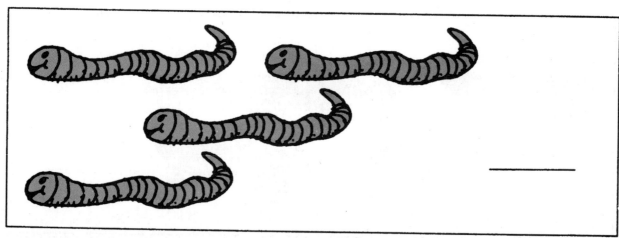

_____

_____

Skills: Counting; Writing numerals

Working with Numbers

Look at the pictures in each box.
How many vehicles are there?
Write the number.

_____

_____

_____

Skills: Counting; Writing numerals

309

Working with Numbers

How many hats are in each box?
Circle the correct number.

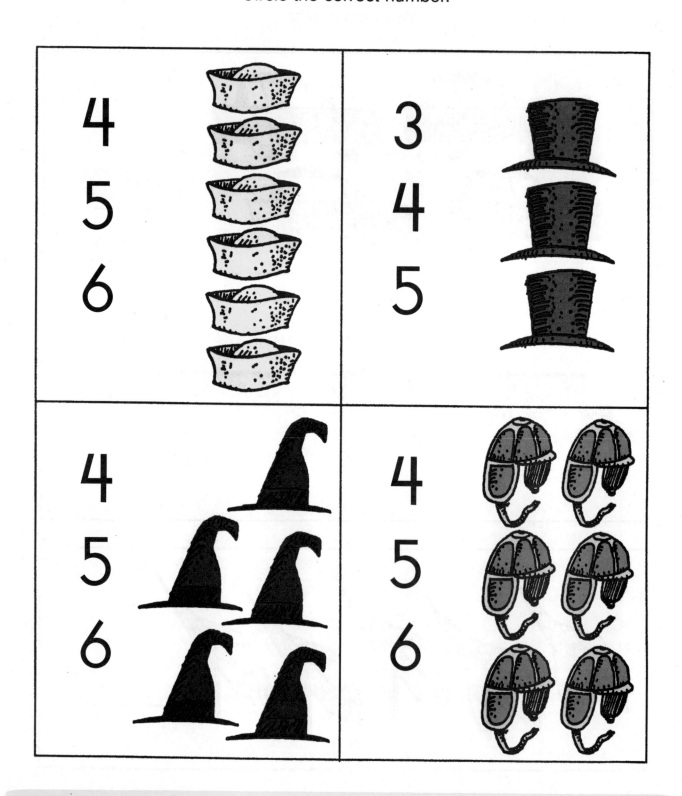

Working with Numbers

How many animals are in each box?
Circle the correct number.

5
6
7

2
3
4

4
5
6

5
6
7

Working with Numbers

How many things are in each box?
Circle the correct number.

5
6
7

8
9
10

8
9
10

7
8
9

Working with Numbers

How many piggy banks are above the line? _____
How many piggy banks are below the line? _____
How many are there in all? _____
Write the number.

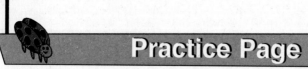

Practice Page

Use this page and the following pages to draw groups of things.
Write the number in each group.

Practice Page

Practice Page

Excellent!

Give yourself a star!

Achievement Checklist

Use the checklist below after each session with this book. If your child had trouble with a page, find the problem skill and list the page number in the middle column. You will want to return to it later. If your child successfully completed the pages containing a skill, put a check mark in the "Mastered" column. Your child can watch with pride as the column fills up with skills he or she has mastered.

BASIC SKILLS	Needs Work	Mastered!
BEGINNING WRITING		
Fine motor skills		
Eye/hand coordination		
Forming vertical lines		
Forming diagonal lines		
Forming open curves		
Forming closed curves		
Forming horizontal lines		
LEARNING LETTERS		
Forming upper/lowercase Aa		
Forming upper/lowercase Bb		
Forming upper/lowercase Cc		
Forming upper/lowercase Dd		
Forming upper/lowercase Ee		
Forming upper/lowercase Ff		
Forming upper/lowercase Gg		
Forming upper/lowercase Hh		
Forming upper/lowercase Ii		
Forming upper/lowercase Jj		
Forming upper/lowercase Kk		
Forming upper/lowercase Ll		
Forming upper/lowercase Mm		
Forming upper/lowercase Nn		
Forming upper/lowercase Oo		
Forming upper/lowercase Pp		
Forming upper/lowercase Qq		
Forming upper/lowercase Rr		
Forming upper/lowercase Ss		
Forming upper/lowercase Tt		
Forming upper/lowercase Uu		
Forming upper/lowercase Vv		
Forming upper/lowercase Ww		
Forming upper/lowercase Xx		
Forming upper/lowercase Yy		
Forming upper/lowercase Zz		
READING READINESS		
Visual discrimination		
Matching		
Association/Classification		
Logical reasoning		
Noticing details		
Following directions		

Achievement Checklist

BASIC SKILLS	Needs Work	Mastered!
READING READINESS		
Understanding directionality		
Word recognition		
Vocabulary		
Opposites		
Patterns		
Visual memory		
BEGINNING PHONICS		
Sound/symbol association		
Auditory discrimination		
Beginning consonants		
Final consonants		
WORDS THAT RHYME		
Recognizing rhyming words		
Word family — ot		
Word family — at		
Word family — ug		
Word family — ake		
Word family — own		
Word family — ing		
COLORS AND SHAPES		
Distinguishing colors: red		
Distinguishing colors: yellow		
Distinguishing colors: blue		
Distinguishing colors: green		
Distinguishing colors: orange		
Distinguishing colors: purple		
Distinguishing colors: brown		
Distinguishing colors: black		
Sight vocabulary		
Matching colors to color words		
Shape recognition		
MATH READINESS SKILLS		
Recognizing position		
Making comparisons		
One-to-one correspondence		
Developing number sense		
Recognizing left and right		
Ordinal numbers		
NUMBER CONCEPTS		
Recognizing sets		
Writing numerals		
Writing number words		
Number order		
WORKING WITH NUMBERS		
Counting		

Diploma

Awarded to

_____

for extraordinary achievement in Getting Ready For Preschool
Basic Skills on this date,

_____

CONGRATULATIONS!